DISCOURSES

by

Meher Baba

Volume III

Mastery in
Servitude

ISBN 0-9774953-0-2

Library of Congress Control Number 2005935268

The sixth edition of Meher Baba's *Discourses* was first printed in 1967. This reprinting is made by the Discourses by Meher Baba Foundation, a not-for-profit organization dedicated to the preservation of the words Meher Baba published during His lifetime.

Quotation on back cover taken from *The Travail of the New World Order.*

Discourses by Meher Baba Foundation
http://www.discoursesbymeherbaba.org/books/index.htm

Meher Baba dictated the *Discourses* on an alphabet board between 1938 and 1943. During those years, at least one discourse appeared in each issue of the monthly "Meher Baba Journal," published in India. Close disciples transcribed Baba's dictations, and Baba signed His name to each transcription to indicate His approval for publication. Between 1939 and 1954, a five-volume compilation of the *Discourses* had several printings, also in India. In 1967, two years before dropping His body, Baba supervised the editing and publication of the *Discourses* in three-volumes, known as the sixth edition. This republication of the sixth edition brings to a new generation the words and form of the *Discourses* Meher Baba last approved during His lifetime.

Introduction

MERWAN Sheriar Irani was born in Poona, India, on February 25, 1894. His parents were of Persian extraction. His father, Sheriar Irani, was a persistent seeker of God.

Merwan was a lively and happy boy who excelled in both studies and sports. In 1913 while in his first year at Poona's Deccan College he met the aged Muslim saint Hazrat Babajan, one of the five Perfect Masters of the time. Being attracted to her, he visited her from time to time and one day she kissed him on the forehead, revealing to him his state of God-realization.

At first Merwan was dazed but gradually the focus of his consciousness returned sufficiently to his surroundings to lead him to the *Qutub-i-Irshad*, Sai Baba, who in turn sent him to another Perfect Master, the Hindu, Upasni Maharaj of Sakori. For seven years Upasni Maharaj integrated Merwan's God-consciousness with consciousness of the mundane world, preparing him for his role as the Avatar of the Age. This avataric mission started in 1921 with the gathering together of his first disciples, who gave him the name "Meher Baba" or "Compassionate Father."

After years of intensive work with these disciples, and travel in India and Persia (Iran), Meher Baba established quarters at an old military camp near

Ahmednagar. This became known as Meherabad. Here he instituted a number of pilot plant projects such as a free hospital and dispensary, shelters for the poor and a free school where spiritual training was stressed. In the school no caste lines were observed, as the high and the low mingled in common fellowship forged by love of the Master. To all Baba offered regular instruction in moral discipline, love for God, spiritual understanding and selfless service.

All these activities moved at high speed despite Baba's silence, which he announced with little advance warning and commenced on July 10, 1925. At first he communicated by pointing to letters on an alphabet board, but in 1954 he gave up even this device. He now converses through his own unique shorthand system of representative gestures. Both *Discourses* and *God Speaks,* however, were dictated on the alphabet board.

During the early 1930's Baba's travels began to reach into Europe and then on to America. Contacting literally thousands on both continents, his name rapidly became known to those deeply and sincerely interested in the spiritual disciplines. Some of these he selected into small groups, arranging for them to come later to India. Their visits ranged generally from weeks to years, but before and during World War II all but a small handful were sent back to their homes.

After the war his own travels resumed, but visits of Westerners to India were now normally individual and brief. An exception was the great East-West gathering of November 1962. Thousands of his devotees from all over the world converged on Poona by ship, plane and special trains. For almost a week Baba gave unstintingly of himself in mass darshans, group meetings and personal interviews. The fare was as varied as the assemblage: brief discourses, give and take with old friends, song in praise of God, prayers, embracing the close ones, a day of mass darshan and crowds storming the gates at sunset. The world's literature contains many references to the need for transfusion between East and West. Here was a rich human stew of contrasting elements in which mutual respect, affection and unity in praise of the Loved One bridged vast differences in tradition.

A persistent theme throughout the five decades of Meher Baba's ministration has been his seeking out of the God-intoxicated and his homage to those lamed by disease and want. He has described most clearly through Dr. William Donkin in *The Wayfarers* the difference between those who have lost touch with creation through insanity and those who have merely turned the focus of their hearts to their vision of God. These latter he terms *masts*. Especially in the 1940's, Meher Baba contacted hundreds of these God-intoxicated souls throughout India, often tending personally to their most intimate needs, giving each what only he might know to be required, and returning them finally to their natural surroundings.

Those stricken by leprosy have been a constant concern of Baba. With infinite care and love he washes their feet, bows his forehead to the often twisted stumps on which they hobble, and sends them on their way with renewed hope and peace. "They are like beautiful birds caught in an ugly cage," he once said on such an occasion. "Of all the tasks I have to perform, this touches me most deeply."

While Baba has travelled widely and contacted millions of people, he emphasizes that he has come not to teach, but to awaken. He states that Truth has been given by the great Messengers of the past, and that the present task of humanity is to *realize* the teaching embodied in each of the great Ways. Baba's mission is to awaken man to that realization through the age-old message of love.

Baba also provides the ready example when one is faced by a puzzling decision. In essence, however, one does not know how Baba achieves the results he so clearly elicits from the human instrument. All that the individual senses is a powerful force sweeping through the snarls of life, simplifying and freeing the inner being in a manner that he instinctively trusts.

One of the great wonders of contact with Baba is acceptance. "He invites people to look at themselves, to accept their egotistic selves not as good or bad, clever or stupid, successful or unsuccessful, but as illusions of their true selves, and to cease to identify themselves with the illusion."

The history of man's search for his soul has produced few works dealing with the technique for the soul's discovery. Meher Baba's *Discourses* are a major contribution to that small body of literature. In this work, given to his close disciples in the period 1938-1943, he describes the means for incorporating daily life into one's spiritual ongoing. He also outlines the structure of Creation, but only to clarify the relationship of the aspirant to the Master. In his classic later work, *God Speaks*, Meher Baba describes in detail the vertical system of God, His will to know Himself consciously, and the purpose of Creation in that will-to-consciousness. The *Discourses* on the other hand are the practical guide for the aspirant as he slowly finds his way back to Oneness, after having developed consciousness through the deeps of evolution.

While the *Discourses* provide detailed descriptions

of the Path and its disciplines, the reader will discover that they are in no way a do-it-yourself manual for spiritual evolution. Rather, they are a constant, firm reminder of the need for a Master on this Path of apparent return to Oneness. The Master is the knowing guide who has already traversed the Path, who provides with infinite patience the security and steady pace that can lead to the goal. While Baba admits the possibility of achieving progress without such a guide, he makes it clear that it is fraught with almost insurmountable problems.

To one who debates allying himself with a teacher of the inner processes, the *Discourses* provide invaluable insight. To one who senses that life is to be lived for its positive contribution to the discovery of the inner being, Baba provides the unarguable description of one who knows.

"These discourses cover a wide field, but they begin and end with the reader himself. This is therefore a dangerous book. Baba is dangerous, as all who have been near him know . . . . Baba invites those who listen to him to do the impossible because only the impossible has divine meaning."

Meher Baba lives quietly in the midst of the greatest activity, often raising an almost impenetrable barrier to guard the seclusion in which he performs his universal work, near Ahmednagar. On occasion he allows individuals and small groups to penetrate the barrier to receive the spark of love, more rarely he opens the gates wide and loosens a broad river of warmth on those who are lucky enough to know that the Avatar is in the world.

Ivy Oneita Duce & Don E. Steven, Editors
1967

Volume I
Contents

Volume II
Contents

Volume II Contents Continued

Volume III
Contents

Volume III Contents Continued

The Avatar

CONSCIOUSLY or unconsciously, every living creature seeks one thing. In the lower forms of life and in less advanced human beings, the quest is unconscious; in advanced human beings, it is conscious. The object of the quest is called by many names—happiness, peace, freedom, truth, love, perfection, Self-realisation, God-realisation, union with God. Essentially, it is a search for all of these, but in a special way. Everyone has moments of happiness, glimpses of truth, fleeting experiences of union with God; what they want is to make them permanent. They want to establish an abiding reality in the midst of constant change.

It is a natural desire, based fundamentally on a memory, dim or clear as the individual's evolution may be low or high, of his essential unity with God; for, every living thing is a partial manifestation of God, conditioned only by its lack of knowledge of its own true nature. The whole of evolution, in fact, is an evolution from unconscious divinity to conscious divinity, in which God Himself, essentially eternal and unchangeable, assumes an infinite variety of forms, enjoys an infinite variety of experiences and transcends an infinite variety of self-imposed limitations. Evolution from the standpoint of the Creator is a divine sport, in which the Unconditioned tests the infinitude of His absolute knowledge, power and bliss in the midst of all conditions. But evolution from the standpoint of the creature, with his limited knowledge, limited power, limited capacity for enjoying bliss, is an epic of alternating rest and struggle, joy and sorrow, love and hate, until, in the perfected man, God balances the pairs of opposites and transcends duality. Then creature and Creator recognise themselves as one; changelessness is established in the midst of change, eternity is experienced in the midst of time. God knows Himself as God, unchangeable in essence, infinite in manifestation, ever experiencing the supreme bliss of Self-realisation in continually fresh awareness of Himself by Himself.

This realisation must and does take place only in the midst of life, for it is only in the midst of life that limitation can be experienced and transcended, and that subsequent freedom from limitation can be enjoyed. This freedom from limitation assumes three forms:

Most God-realised souls leave the body at once and forever, and remain eternally merged in the unmanifest aspect of God. They are conscious only of the bliss of union. Creation no longer exists for them. Their constant round of births and deaths is ended. This is known as *mukti* or liberation.

Some God-realised souls retain the body for a time, but their consciousness is merged completely in the unmanifest aspect of God, and they are therefore not conscious either of their bodies or of creation. They experience constantly the infinite bliss, power and knowledge of God, but they cannot consciously use them in creation or help others to attain to liberation. Nevertheless, their presence on earth is like a focal point for the concentration and radiation of the infinite power, knowledge and bliss of God; and those who approach them, serve them and worship them are spiritually benefited by contact with them. These souls are called *Majzubs,* and this particular type of liberation is called *videh-mukti* or liberation with the body.

A few God-realised souls keep the body, yet are conscious of themselves as God in both His unmanifest and His manifest aspects. They know themselves both as the unchangeable divine essence and as the infinitely varied manifestation. They experience themselves as God apart from creation, as God the Creator, Preserver and Destroyer of the whole of creation, and as God Who has accepted and transcended the limitations of creation. They experience constantly the absolute peace, the infinite knowledge, power and bliss of God. They enjoy to the full the divine sport of creation. They know themselves as God in everything, and are therefore able to help everything spiritually, and to make other souls realise God, either as *Muktas, Majzubs* or *Sadgurus* as they themselves are called.

There are fifty-six God-realised souls in the world at all times. They are always one in consciousness. They are always different in function. For the most part they live and work apart from and unknown to the general public, but five, who act in a sense as a directing body, always work in public and attain to public prominence and importance. These are known as *Sadgurus* or Perfect Masters. In *Avataric* periods, the *Avatar,* as a supreme *Sadguru,* takes his place as the head of this body and of the spiritual hierarchy as a whole.

Avataric periods are like the spring-tide of creation. They bring a new release of power, a new awakening of consciousness, a new experience of life—not merely for a few, but for all. Qualities of energy and awareness, which had been used and enjoyed by only a few advanced souls, are made available for all humanity. Life, as a whole, is stepped up to a higher level of consciousness, is geared to a new rate of energy. The transition from sensation to reason was one such step; the transition from reason to intuition will be another.

This new influx of the creative impulse takes, through the medium of a divine personality, an incarnation of God in a special sense—the *Avatar.* This *Avatar* was the first individual soul to emerge from the evolutionary process as a *Sadguru,* and he is the only *Avatar* who has ever manifested or will ever manifest. Through him God first completed the journey from unconscious divinity to conscious divinity, first unconsciously became man in order consciously to become God. Through him, periodically, God consciously becomes man for the liberation of mankind.

The *Avatar* appears in different forms, under different names, at different times, in different parts of the world. As his appearance always coincides with the spiritual birth of man, so the period immediately preceding his manifestation is always one in which humanity suffers from the pangs of the approaching birth. Man seems more than ever enslaved by desire, more than ever driven by greed, held by fear, swept by anger. The strong dominate the weak; the rich oppress the poor; large masses of people are exploited for the benefit of the few who are in power. The individual, who finds no peace or rest, seeks to forget himself in excitement. Immorality increases, crime flourishes, religion is ridiculed. Corruption spreads throughout the social order. Class and national hatreds are aroused and fostered. Wars break out. Humanity grows desperate. There seems to be no possibility of stemming the tide of destruction.

At this moment the *Avatar* appears. Being the total manifestation of God in human form, he is like a gauge against which man can measure what he is and what he may become. He trues the standard of human values by interpreting them in terms of divinely human life.

He is interested in everything but not concerned about anything. The slightest mishap may command his sympathy; the greatest tragedy will not upset him. He is beyond the alternations of pain and pleasure, desire and satisfaction, rest and struggle, life and death. To him they are equally illusions which he has transcended, but by which others are bound, and from which he has come to free them. He uses every circumstance as a means to lead others towards Realisation.

He knows that men do not cease to exist when they die, and therefore is not concerned over death. He knows that destruction must precede construction, that out of suffering is born peace and bliss, that out of struggle comes liberation from the bonds of action. He is only concerned about concern.

In those who contact him he awakens a love that consumes all selfish desires in the flame of the one desire to serve him. Those who consecrate their lives to him gradually become identified with him in consciousness. Little by little, their humanity is absorbed into his divinity and they become free.

Those who are closest to him are known as his circle. Every *Sadguru* has an intimate circle of twelve disciples who, in point of realisation, are made equal to the *Sadguru* himself, though they differ from him in function and authority. In *Avataric* periods the *Avatar* has a circle of one hundred and twenty disciples, all of whom experience realisation and work for the liberation of others.*

Their work is not only for contemporary humanity but for posterity as well. The unfoldment of life and consciousness for the whole *Avataric* cycle, which has been mapped out in the creative world before the *Avatar* took form, is endorsed and fixed in the formative and material worlds during the *Avatar*'s life on earth.

The *Avatar* awakens contemporary humanity to a realisation of its true spiritual nature, gives liberation to those who are ready, and quickens the life of the spirit in his time. For posterity is left the stimulating power of his divinely human example, the nobility of a life supremely lived, of a love unmixed with desire, of a power unused except for others, of a peace untroubled by ambition, of a knowledge undimmed by illusion. He has demonstrated the possibility of a divine life for all humanity, of a heavenly life on earth. Those who have the necessary courage and integrity can follow when they will.

Those who are spiritually awake have been aware for some time that the world is at present in the midst of a period such as always precedes *Avataric* manifestations. Even unawakened men and women are becoming aware of it now. From their darkness they are reaching out for light; in their sorrow they are longing for comfort; from the midst of the strife into which they have found themselves plunged, they are praying for peace and deliverance.

For the moment they must be patient. The wave of destruction must rise still higher, must spread still further. But when, from the depths of his heart, man desires something more lasting than wealth, something

*For further description see *Civilisation or Chaos* by Irene Conybeare (Chetna, Bombay) or Vol. 3, No. 1 *The Awakener.*

more real than material power, the wave will recede. Then peace will come, joy will come, light will come.

The breaking of my silence—the signal for my public manifestation—is not far off. I bring the greatest treasure which it is possible for man to receive—a treasure which includes all other treasures, which will endure forever, which increases when shared with others. Be ready to receive it.

The Travail of the New World Order

THE world-storm which has been gathering momentum is now having its greatest outburst*, and in reaching its climax it will work universal disaster. In

World-storm

the struggle for material well-being, all grievances have assumed fantastic proportions, and the diverse differences of human interest have been so accentuated that they have precipitated distinctive conflict. Humanity has failed to solve its individual and social problems, and the evidence for this failure is very clear. The incapacity of men to deal with their problems constructively and creatively reveals a *tragic deficiency in the right understanding of the basic nature of man and the true purpose of life.*

The world is witnessing an acute *conflict between the forces of Light and the forces of Darkness.* On the one hand there are selfish persons who seek their hap-

Conflict between forces of light and darkness

piness blindly through lust for power, unbridled greed and unrelieved hatred. Ignorant of the real purpose of life, they have

---

* Originally written and published in 1941-1942.

sunk down to the lowest level of culture. They bury their higher selves in the wreckage of crumbling forms which linger on from the dead past. Bound by material interests and limited conceptions, they are *forgetful of their divine destiny.* They have lost their way, and their hearts are torn by the ravages of hate and rancour. On the other hand there are persons who unveil their inherent higher selves through the endurance of pain and deprivation and through noble acts of bravery and self-sacrifice. The present war is teaching man to be brave, to be able to suffer, to understand and to sacrifice.

The disease of selfishness in mankind will need a cure which is not only universal in its application but drastic in nature. It is so deep-rooted that it can be eradicated only if it is attacked **Need for cure of** from all sides. *Real peace and* **selfishness** *happiness will dawn spontaneously when there is a purging of selfishness. The peace and happiness which come from self-giving love are permanent.* Even the worst sinners can become great saints if they have the courage and sincerity to invite a drastic and complete change of heart.

The present chaos and destruction will engulf the whole world, but this will be followed by a very long period in which there shall be no war. The passing **Man will be sick of** sufferings and miseries of our **wanting, greed and** times will be worth enduring **hate** for the sake of the long period of happiness which is to follow. What will the present chaos lead to? How will it all end? It can only end in one way. Mankind will be sick of it all. Men will be sick of wanting and sick of fighting out of hatred. Greed and hatred will reach such intensity that everyone will become weary of them. The way out of the dead-lock will be found through selflessness. *The only alternative which can bring a solution will be to stop hating and to love, to stop wanting and to give, to stop dominating and to serve.*

Great suffering awakens great understanding. Supreme suffering fulfills its purpose and yields its true significance when it awakens exhausted human-

Suffering shall gener-ate understanding

ity and stirs within it a genuine longing for real understanding. *Unprecedented suffering leads to unprecedented spiritual growth. It contributes to the construction of life on the unshakable foundation of the Truth.* It is now high time that universal suffering should hasten humanity to the turning point in its spiritual history. It is now high time that the very agonies of our times should become a medium for bringing a real un-derstanding of human relationship. It is now high time for humanity to face squarely the true causes of the catastrophe which has overtaken it. It is now high time to seek a new experience of Reality. To know that life is real and eternal is to inherit unfading bliss. It is time that men had this realisation by being unified with their own selves.

Through unification with the higher self, man per-ceives the Infinite Self in all selves. He becomes free by outgrowing and discarding the limitations of the ego-

Affirmation of the Truth of Oneness

life. *The individual soul has to realise with full consciousness its identity with the Universal Soul.* Men shall reorient life in the light of this ancient Truth, and they will readjust their attitude towards their neighbours in everyday life. To perceive the spiritual val-ue of *oneness* is to promote real unity and co-operation. Brotherhood then becomes a spontaneous outcome of true perception. *The new life which is based upon spiritual understanding is an affirmation of the Truth.* It is not something which belongs to utopia, but is completely practical. Now that humanity is thrown into the fire of bloody conflicts, through immense anguish it is experiencing the utter instability and futility of the life which is based upon purely material conceptions. The hour is near when men in their eager longing for real happiness will seek its true source.

The time is also ripe when men will ardently seek to contact the embodiment of Truth in the form of a God-Man, through whom they can be inspired and lifted into

Inherit Divine love through God-Man

spiritual understanding. They will accept the guidance which comes from divine authority. Only the outpouring of divine love can bring about spiritual awakening. In this critical time of universal suffering, men are becoming ready to turn towards their Higher Self and to fulfill the will of God. Divine love will perform the supreme miracle of bringing God into the hearts of men and of getting them established in lasting and true happiness. It will satisfy the greatest need and longing of mankind. Divine love will make men selfless and helpful in their mutual relations, and it will bring about the final solution of all problems. *The new brotherhood on earth shall be a fulfilled fact and nations will be united in the fraternity of Love and Truth.*

My existence is for this Love and this Truth. To suffering humanity I say:

"*Have hope.* I have come to help you in surrendering yourselves to the Cause of God and in accepting His grace of Love and Truth. I have come to help you in winning the one victory of all victories—to win yourself."

The Man-God

PART I

ASPIRANTS AND GOD-REALISED BEINGS

E VEN before God-realisation, the advanced aspirants pass through states of consciousness which, in some ways, are akin to the state of God-realisation. *For*

The joy of God-intoxication

example, the Masts and saints of the higher planes are completely desireless and immersed in the joy of God-intoxication. Since their only concern is God, they become the recipients of the unique happiness which is characteristic of the God-state. They have no Beloved except God, and they have no longing except for God. For them, God is not only the only Beloved, but also the only Reality that counts. They are unattached to everything except God, and remain unaffected by the pleasures and the pains to which worldly persons are subject, and they are happy because they are always face to face with the Divine Beloved, Who is the very ocean of happiness.

Advanced aspirants not only participate in some of the privileges of the Divine State, but also wield great

Powers of advanced aspirants

occult powers and *Siddhis.* Depending upon the point of view of the powers which they wield, the aspirants belong to different types. For example, even on the first plane the aspirant begins to see lights and colours, smell perfumes and hear the music of the subtle world. Those who advance further can see and hear things at any distance. Some aspirants see the whole gross world as a mirage. Some advanced aspirants can take a new body immediately after their death. Some agents of Perfect Masters have such control over the gross world that they can change their bodies at will. In Sufi tradition they are called *Abdals*. All these achievements of aspirants pertain to the phenomenal world. The field of their powers is itself a domain of illusion, and the miracles which they perform do not necessarily mean that they are in any way nearer to the God-state.

From the standpoint of *consciousness* also, aspirants belong to various types according to the line in which they have advanced and according to their nearness to the God-state. Some get intoxicated with their extraordinary powers and, tempted to use them, have a long pause in their Godward march.

Different states of aspirants

They get stuck in the consciousness of the intermediate planes. Some become dazed, confused and even self-deluded. Some are caught in a coma. There are some who, with difficulty, try to come down to gross consciousness by repeating some physical action or by repeating a sentence many times. There are some who, in their God-intoxication, are so indifferent to the life of the gross world that to all appearances their external behaviour is like that of mad persons. And there are some who tread the Path while performing their worldly duties.

Owing to their exalted states of consciousness, some advanced aspirants are adorable, but they are in no way comparable to God-realised persons, either in

Unmatta state

spiritual beauty and perfection of the inward state of consciousness, or in their powers. All aspirants, right up to the sixth plane, are limited by finite consciousness, and they are all in the domain of duality and illusion. Aspirants are mostly happy: it is due to their contact and communion with God. For some the joy of inward companionship with the Divine Beloved is so great that they become unbalanced in their behaviour. As a result, in their *unsubdued state of God-intoxication* they may abuse people, throw stones at them and behave like ghosts. Their state is often described as that of the *Unmatta. Owing to the exuberance of uncontrolled joy in their inward contact with the Divine Beloved, they are utterly heedless of worldly standards or values.* Owing to the fearlessness which comes to them through complete detachment, they often manifest a self-expression which can easily be mistaken for idiosyncracy and unruliness.

Only when it attains God-realisation on the seventh plane can the soul fully control its joy. *The unlimited happiness which is eternally his does not in any way un-*

Complete poise only on seventh plane

balance the person because he is now permanently established in the poise of non-duality. The extravagance of newly found love and joy is no longer for him. Occasional unsettlement due to increasing joy at the closer proximity of God is also finished because he is now inseparably united with Him. He is lost in the Divine Beloved and merged into Him, Who is the infinite ocean of unbounded happiness.

The happiness of the God-realised person is unconditioned and self-sustained. It is therefore eternally the same, without ebb and flow. He has arrived at unquali-

Happiness of God-realised is Self-sustained

fied finality and unassailable equanimity. *The happiness of the saints is born of increasing proximity and closer intimacy* with the Divine Beloved Who, however, remains an externalised Another. *The happiness of the God-realised, however, is an inalienable aspect of the God-state, in which there is no duality. The happiness of the saints is derivative, but the happiness of the God-realised is self-grounded.* The happiness of the saints comes from increasing bounty of Divine Grace, but the happiness of the God-realised merely IS.

When a person attains God-realisation he has infinite power, knowledge and bliss. These intrinsic characteristics of inner realisation are always the same despite

Differences in relation to universe

minor side-differences which give rise to certain distinguishable types of God-realised persons. These differences between the God-realised are purely extrinsic and pertain only to their relation with the universe. They do not create any degrees of spiritual status between the God-realised, who are all perfect and one with all life and existence.

From the point of view of the creation, however, these differences between God-realised persons are not only definite but worth noting. After God-realisation,

Some God-realised beings drop body

some souls *drop all their bodies* and remain eternally immersed in God-consciousness. For them, God is the only reality and the entire universe is a zero. They are so completely identified with the impersonal aspect of the Truth that they have no direct link with the world of forms.

Some God-realised souls retain their gross, subtle and mental bodies, but in their absorption of God-consciousness, they are totally unconscious of the existence of their bodies. Other souls in creation might continue to see their bodies and treat them as persons incarnate, but these bodies exist only from the point of view of the observer. Such God-realised persons are called *Majzubs* in Sufi terminology. The *Majzubs* do not use their bodies consciously, because their consciousness is wholly directed towards God and is not turned towards the bodies or the universe. For them their own bodies as well as the world of forms have no existence, so there can be no question of their using the bodies in relation to the world of forms. However, their bodies are necessarily the centres for the radiation of the unpremeditated and constant overflow of the infinite bliss, knowledge and love which they enjoy. Those who revere these bodies derive great spiritual benefit from this spontaneous radiation of divinity.

Majzubs

Some God-realised persons have, in addition to consciousness of God, an awareness of the existence of other souls who are in bondage. They know all these souls to be forms of the *Paramatma* who are all destined one day to achieve emancipation and God-realisation. Being established in this knowledge, they remain indifferent to the provisional and changing lots of the souls who are in bondage. These God-realised souls know that, just as they themselves have realised God, others will also realise God at some time. They are in no hurry to speed up the God-realisation of those who are in bondage, and take *no active interest in the time-process of creation.*

Some God-realised souls uninterested in creation

Some God-realised souls not only possess God-consciousness, but are also conscious of creation and their own bodies. They take active interest in the souls

Sadguru (Man-God)

who are in bondage, and *they use their own bodies consciously to work in creation, in order to help other souls in their God-ward march.* Such a God-realised soul is called a *Salik, Sadguru* or *Man-God.* The Salik or Sadguru finds himself in the centre of the entire universe, and everyone, high or low, good or bad, is at the same distance from him. In the Sufi tradition, this *centre* is called the *Qutub.* The Qutub controls the whole universe through his agents.

The foremost Sadguru who first emerged through evolution, and helped and helps other souls in bondage, is known as the Avatar. There is another difference

Avatar (God-Man)

between the Sadguru and the Avatar. When man becomes God and has creation-consciousness, he is called Sadguru (Man-God or Perfect Master). When God becomes man, he is called Avatar (God-Man or Messiah).

From the point of view of fundamental characteristics of consciousness and the nature of the work in creation, the Avatar is like any other Sadguru (Man-God). Neither the Avatar nor the Sadguru has a finite and limited mind, because after merging in the Infinite the mind becomes universal. The Salik or Sadguru or Man-God, as well as the Avatar, do not lose their God-consciousness even for a moment, although they may be engaged in all sorts of activities in relation to creation. *Both work through the universal mind, which is theirs, when they desire to help other souls.*

The Man-God

Part II
THE STATE OF THE MAN-GOD

OF all the objects of human study, God is the best. But purely theoretical study of God does not take the aspirant very far towards the real purpose of human life, though it is always

Realising God different from intellecual knowledge of God

better to study God than to be completely ignorant of His existence. He who seeks God intellectually is infinitely better than the person who is merely a skeptic or an agnostic. But it is decidedly better to feel God than to study Him through the intellect, though even feeling for God is less important than the actual experience of God. However, even the experience of God does not yield the true nature of Divinity, because God, as the object of experience, remains different from and external to the aspirant. The true nature of God is known to the aspirant only when he attains unity with God, by losing himself in His Being. *Thus, it is better to study God than to be ignorant of Him; it is better to feel God than to study Him; it is better to experience God than to feel God; and it is better to become God than to experience Him.*

The state of God-realisation is unmarred by doubts

which cloud the minds of those who are in bondage. Those in bondage are in a constant state of uncertainty

Supreme certainty

about their "whence" and "whither." The God-realised, on the other hand, are at the very heart of creation where its source and end are known. The God-realised person knows himself to be God as surely as ordinary man knows himself to be a man and not a dog. For him it is not a matter of doubt, belief, self-delusion or guess-work. It is a matter of supreme and unshakable certainty which needs no external corroborations, and remains unaffected by the contradiction of others, because it is based upon continuous Self-knowledge. His spiritual certainty cannot be challenged by anyone or anything. He cannot think of himself as anything but God, just as ordinary man cannot think of himself as being anything except man. But the man thinks himself to be what he is not in reality, and the God-realised knows himself to be what he is in reality.

God-realisation is the very goal of all creation. All earthly pleasure, however great, is but a fleeting shadow of the eternal bliss of God-realisation. All mundane

Glory of God-realisation

knowledge, however comprehensive, is but a distorted reflection of the Absolute Truth of God-realisation. All human might, however imposing, is but a fragment of the infinite power of God-realisation. *All that is noble, beautiful and lovely, all that is great, good and inspiring in the universe, is just an infinitesimal fraction of the unfading and unspeakable glory of God-realisation.*

The eternal bliss, the Absolute Truth, the infinite power and the unfading glory of God-realisation, are not to be had for nothing. The individualised soul has to

Price of God-realisation

go through all the travail of the pain and struggle of evolution (and reincarnations) before it can inherit this Treasure, which is hidden at the heart of creation, and the price which it has to pay for coming into possession of this Treasure is its own existence as a separate ego. The limited individuality must disappear entirely if there is to be an entrance into the unlimited state of God-hood. In the ordinary man of the world, the limited individuality, which is identified with a finite name and form, predominates and creates a veil of ignorance over the God within. If this ignorance is to disappear, the limited individual has to surrender his own limited existence. When he goes from the scene without leaving a vestige of his limited life, what remains is God. *The surrenderance of limited existence is the surrenderance of a firmly rooted delusion of having a separate existence. It is not the surrenderance of anything real: it is the surrenderance of the false and the inheritance of the Truth.*

When a person is crossing the inner planes towards God-realisation, he becomes successively unconscious of the gross, subtle and mental worlds as well as his

Two aspects of Man-God

own gross, subtle and mental bodies. But after God-realisation, some souls again descend or come down and become conscious of the whole creation as well as their gross, subtle and mental bodies, without in any way jeopardising their God-consciousness. They are known as Perfect Masters. *God as God alone is not consciously man, and man as man alone is not consciously God; the Man-God is consciously God as well as man.*

By again becoming conscious of creation, the

Man-God does not suffer the slightest deterioration of his spiritual status. What is spiritually disastrous is not

Man-God not caught up in creation

mere consciousness of creation, but the fact that consciousness is *caught up* in creation because of the *sanskaras.* Consequently it is covered with ignorance, and this prevents the realisation of the Divinity within. In the same way, what is spiritually disastrous is not mere consciousness of the bodies, but *identification* with them due to the *sanskaras.* These prevent the realisation of the Infinite Soul, which is the ultimate Reality and the ground of all creation. In it alone is to be found the final meaning of the entire creation.

The soul in bondage is tied to the worlds of forms by the chain of *sanskaras,* which create the illusion of identification of the soul with the bodies. *The disharmony within consciousness and the perversions in the expression of the will arise from sansakaric identification with the bodies and not merely through consciousness of the bodies.* Since the Man-God is free from all *sanskaras,* he is constantly conscious of being different from the bodies and uses them harmoniously as mere *instruments* for the expression of the Divine Will in all its purity. The bodies are to the Man-God what the wig is to the bald man. The bald man puts on his wig when he goes to work during the day, and he takes it off when he retires at night. So the Man-God uses his bodies when he needs them for his work, but is free of them when he does not need them, and knows them to be utterly different from his true being as God.

The Man-God knows himself to be infinite and beyond all forms, and with complete detachment can therefore remain conscious of creation, without being caught up in it. The falseness of the phenomenal

**Changing shadow of
God cannot affect
God-consciousness**

world consists in its not being understood properly, *i.e.*, as being an illusory expression of the Infinite Spirit. Ignorance consists in taking the form as complete in itself, without any reference to the Infinite Spirit of which it is the expression. *The Man-God realises the Truth. He is conscious of the true nature of God as well as the true nature of creation, and yet this does not involve him in any consciousness of duality because, for him, creation does not exist as anything but the changing shadow of God, Who is the only Eternal and Real Existence, and Who is at the heart of creation.* The Man-God can, therefore, remain conscious of creation without lessening his God-consciousness, and he continues to work in the world of forms for the furtherance of the primary purpose of creation, which is to create full Self-knowledge or God-realisation in every soul.

When the Man-God descends into the world of forms from the impersonal aspect of God, he gets universal mind, and he knows, feels and works through

**Man-God works
through universal
mind**

this universal mind. No longer for him is the limited life of finite mind; no longer for him are the pains and the pleasures of duality; no longer for him is the emptiness and the vanity of separative ego. He is consciously one with all life. *Through his universal mind he not only experiences the happiness of all minds but also their suffering.* Since most minds have a great preponderance of suffering over happiness due to ignorance, the suffering which thus comes to the Man-God because of the condition of others is infinitely greater than happiness. The suffering of the Man-God is great, but the infinite bliss of the

God-state which he constantly and effortlessly enjoys supports him in all the suffering which comes to him, leaving him unmoved and unaffected by it.*

The individualised soul has no access to the infinite bliss of the God-state, and he is seriously moved and affected by his sanskaric happiness and suffering because of his ignorant identification with the limited mind. The Man-God does not identify himself even with the universal

Man-God drops universal mind after his mission

mind which he gets while coming down for the world. He has taken the universal mind only for his mission in the world, and since he uses it solely for his work without identification with it, he remains unaffected by the suffering or happiness which comes to him through it. He drops the universal mind after his work is done; but *even when he is working in the world through his universal mind, he knows himself to be the eternal and only God and not the universal mind.*

The union which the Man-God has with God is perfect. Even when he has come down into duality for his universal work, he is not aloof from God even for a second. In his normal state as man, he has to be on the level of all and eat, drink and suffer

Man-God not affected by suffering

like others, but as he retains his Godhood even while he does all these things, he constantly experiences peace, bliss and power. For example, Christ did suffer on the cross, but He was not affected by it because, in the con-

* Many of the statements in these sections apply equally to the God-Man, that unique messenger of God who is called down by the five Perfect Masters once in a cyclic period ranging from 700 to 1400 years. For details, see *God Speaks, by* Meher Baba.

tinuous knowledge which His conscious Godhood gave Him, He knew at the same time that everything in the world of duality is illusion and was sustained by the bliss of union with God.

As God, the Man-God sees all souls as his own. He sees himself in everything and his universal mind includes all minds in its scope. The Man-God knows

Cruxifiction himself to be one with all the other souls in bondage. *Although he knows himself to be identical with God and is thus eternally free, he also knows himself to be one with the other souls in bondage and is thus vicariously bound.* Though he constantly experiences the eternal bliss of God-realisation, he also vicariously experiences suffering owing to the bondage of other souls whom he knows to be his own forms. This is the *meaning of Christ's crucifixion.* The Man-God is, as it were, continuously being crucified, and he is continuously taking birth. In the Man-God, the purpose of creation has been completely realised. He has nothing to obtain for himself by remaining in the world, yet he retains his bodies and continues to use them for emancipating other souls from bondage and helping them to attain God-consciousness.

Even while working in the world of duality, the Man-God is in no way limited by duality. In his God-state, the duality of "I" and "you" is swallowed up in

Non-duality in midst of duality the all-embracing divine love. *The state of perfection in which the Man-God dwells is beyond all forms of duality and opposites. It is a state of unlimited freedom and unimpaired completeness, immortal sweetness and undying happiness, untarnished divinity and unhampered creativity. The Man-God is inseparably united with God forever and dwells in a state of non-dual-*

ity in the very midst of duality. He not only knows himself to be one with all, but also knows himself to be the only one. He consciously descended from the state of seeing nothing but God to the state of seeing God in everything. Therefore, his dealings in the world of duality not only do not bind him, but reflect the pristine glory of the sole Reality, which is God, and contribute towards freeing others from their state of bondage.

The Man-God

Part III
THE WORK OF THE MAN-GOD

*G*OD-REALISATION *is the endless end of creation and the timeless consummation and fructification of intelligent and unbinding Karma.* Souls who have not

Free and unbinding give and take

realised God are still in the domain of duality, and their dealings of mutual give and take in different fields create the chains of *Karmic* debts and dues from which there is no escape. The Man-God however dwells in the consciousness of unity, and all that he does, not only does not bind him, but contributes towards the emancipation of others who are still in ignorance. For the Man-God there is none who is excluded from his own being. He sees himself in everyone, and *since all that he does springs from the consciousness of non-duality, he can freely give and freely take without creating bindings for himself or others.*

If a person accepts without reserve from the bounty which the Man-God showers, he creates a link which will stand by him until he attains the goal of freedom and God-realisation. If a per-

Contact with Man-God beneficial to all

son serves the Man-God, offering all his life and possessions in his service, he creates a link which will augment his spiritual progress by inviting upon himself the grace and help of the Man-God. *In fact, even opposition to the work of the Man-God often turns out to be a beginning of development which imperceptibly leads a person Godward* because, while opposing the work of the Man-God, the soul is establishing a link and a contact with him. Thus everyone who voluntarily or involuntarily comes into the orbit of his activities becomes, in some way, the recipient of a spiritual push.

The work of the Man-God in the universe is fundamentally different from the kind of thing on which most priests set their hearts. Most priests of established

Man-God and priests

religions attach too much importance to external forms, rituals and conformity. Since they themselves are not free from selfishness, narrowness or ignorance, they exploit the weak and the credulous by holding before them the fear of hell or the hope of heaven. The Man-God, on the other hand, has entered forever into the eternal life of love, purity, universality and understanding. He is therefore concerned only with the things that really matter and which eventually bring about the inner unfoldment of spirit in all whom he helps. Those who are themselves in ignorance may, out of self-delusion or deliberate selfishness, use the same language as that of the Man-God, and they may try to imitate the Man-God in many of the external things associated with the life of the Man-God. But they cannot, by the very nature of their spiritual limitations, really imitate the Man-God in possessing perfect understanding, experiencing infinite bliss or wielding unlimited power. These attributes belong to the Man-God by virtue of his having attained unity with God.

Those who are in ignorance lack fundamental traits of the Man-God; and if, out of self-delusion or hypocrisy, they try to pose as the Man-God, their self-

Self-delusion and hypocrisy

delusion or pretence is invariably exposed at some time. If a person gets committed to a way of life out of self-delusion, it is an unfortunate situation. He believes himself to be what he is not and thinks that he knows when he actually does not know. But since he is sincere in all that he thinks or does, he is not to be blamed, though to a limited extent he can become a source of danger to others. The hypocrite knows that he does not know and pretends to be what he is not for selfish reasons. In doing so he creates a serious *Karmic* binding for himself. Though he is a source of considerable danger to the weak and the credulous, he cannot go on indefinitely with his willful deceit, for in the course of time he is automatically exposed by some claim which he is unable to substantiate.

In the performance of his universal work the Man-God has infinite adaptability. He is not attached to any one method of helping others; he does not follow rules

Man-God can play role of aspirant

or precedents, but is a law unto himself. He can rise to any occasion and play the role which is necessary under the circumstances without being bound by it. Once a devotee asked his Master the reason why he fasted. The Master replied, "I am not fasting to attain perfection, for having already attained perfection, I am not an aspirant. It is for the sake of others that I fast." A spiritual aspirant cannot act like one who has attained perfection, since the perfect one is inimitable, but *the perfect one can, for the guidance or benefit of others, act like an aspirant.* One who has passed the highest examination of the university can write the alphabet without difficulty to teach children, but children cannot do what he can do. To show the way to Divinity, the Man-God may often play the role of a devotee of God, though he has attained complete unity with God. He plays the role of a *Bhakta* even after realisation, in order that others may know the way. He is not bound to any particular role, and he can adjust his technique of helping others to the needs of those who seek his guidance. Whatever he does is for the ultimate good of others. For him there is nothing worth obtaining, because he has become everything.

Not only is the Man-God not necessarily bound to any particular technique in giving spiritual help to others, but also he is not bound to the conventional standard of good. He is beyond

Man-God uses *Maya* to annihilate *Maya*

the distinction of good and evil but, although what he does may appear lawless in the eyes of the world, it is always meant for the ultimate good of others. He uses different methods for different persons. He has no self-interest or personal motive and is always inspired by compassion that seeks the true well-being of others. Therefore, in all that he does, he remains unbound. He uses *Maya* to draw his disciples out of *Maya*, and employs infinite ways and workings for his spiritual task. His methods are different with different persons, and they are not the same with the same person at all times. Occasionally he may even do something which shocks others because it runs counter to their usual expectations. However, this is always intended to serve some spiritual purpose. *The intervention of a short shocking dream is often useful in awakening a person from a long beautiful dream.* Like the shocking dream, the shocks which the Man-God in his discretion deliberately administers, are eventually wholesome, although they may be unpleasant at the time.

The Man-God may even seem to be unduly harsh with certain persons, but onlookers have no idea of the internal situation and cannot therefore understand

Saving drowning person

properly the justification of his apparent cruelty. In fact his sternness is often demanded by the spiritual requirements of the situation and is necessary in the best interests of those to whom he seems to be harsh. We have a good and illustrative analogy for such apparently cruel action in the case of an expert swimmer who saves a drowning person. It is well known that if a person is drowning, he has a tendency to cling to anything that comes to hand. In his desperation he is so blind to consequence that his thoughtless grip on the person who has come to save him not only makes it impossible for him to be saved, but is often instrumental in drowning the very person who has come to save him. In fact, an expert in this art of saving drowning persons must often hit the drowning man on the head and render him "unconscious." Through his apparent cruelty he minimises the danger which the drowning man is likely to create, and so ensures success for his efforts. In the same way, the apparent sternness of the Man-God is intended to secure the ultimate spiritual well-being of others.

The soul in bondage is caught up in the universe, and the universe is nothing but imagination. Since there is no end to imagination, he is likely to wander

Cutting short stages of false consciousness

indefinitely in the mazes of false consciousness. The Man-God can help him to *cut short the different stages of false consciousness by revealing the Truth.* When the mind does not perceive the Truth, it is likely to imagine all kinds of things. For example, the soul can imagine that it is a beggar or a king, a man or a woman, etc.

The soul thus goes on gathering experiences of the opposites. Wherever there is duality there is a tendency to restore balance through the opposite. For example,

Seed of God-realisation

if a person has the experience of being a murderer, it has to be counter-balanced by the experience of being murdered; and if the soul has the experience of being a king, it has to be counter-balanced by the experience of being a beggar. Thus *the soul may wander ad infinitum from one opposite to the other without being able to put an end to false consciousness.* The Man-God can help him to arrive at Truth by giving him perception of the Truth and *cutting short the working of his imagination, which would otherwise be endless.* The Man-God helps the soul in bondage by *sowing in him the seed of God-realisation,* but it always takes some time to attain God-realisation. Every process of growth in the universe takes time.

The help of the Man-God is however far more effective than the help which some advanced aspirant may give. When an aspirant helps, he can take a per-

The Help of Man-God

son only up to the point which he himself has reached. Even this limited help which he can give becomes effective very gradually, with the result that the person who ascends through such help has to stay in the first plane for a long time, then in the second and so on. When the Man-God chooses to help a person, he may, through his grace, take the aspirant even to the seventh plane in one second, though in that one second the person has to traverse all the intermediate planes.

In taking a person to the seventh plane the Man-God is making him equal to himself, and the person who thus attains the highest spiritual status himself becomes likewise a Man-God. **Analogy of banyan tree** This transmission of spiritual knowledge from the Man-God to his disciple is comparable to *the lighting of one lamp from another.* The lamp which has been lighted is as capable of giving light to others as the original lamp itself. There is no difference between them in importance or utility. The Man-God is comparable to the banyan tree. *The banyan tree grows huge and mighty, giving shade and shelter to travellers and protecting them from the sun, rain and storm. In the fullness of its growth its descending rooting branches strike deep into the fallow ground to create, in due time, another full-grown banyan tree. It too becomes equally huge and mighty, giving shade and shelter to travellers and protecting them from sun, rain and storm, and has the same potential power to create similar full-grown banyan trees. The same is true of the Man-God, who arouses the Godhood latent in others.* The continued succession of the Perfect Masters on earth is a perpetual blessing to mankind, helping it onward in its struggle through darkness.

The Man-God may be said to be the Lord and servant of the universe at one and the same time. As one who showers his spiritual bounty on all in measureless abundance, he is the Lord of **Lord and servant** the universe. As one who continuously bears the burden of all and helps them through numberless spiritual difficulties, he is the servant of the universe. *Just as he is Lord and servant in one, he is also* *the supreme Lover and the matchless Beloved. The love he gives or receives goes to free the soul from ignorance. In giving love he gives it to himself in other forms; in receiving love he receives what has been awakened through his own Grace, which is continuously showered on all without distinction.* The Grace of the Man-God is like the rain, which falls equally on all lands irrespective of whether they are barren or fertile, but it fructifies only in the lands which have been rendered fertile through arduous and patient toiling.

The Circle

AFTER several lives of search, purification, service and self-sacrifice a soul has the good fortune to meet and get connected with a God-realised Master.

Entering circle of Master

After several lives of close connection with the Master and love and service for the Master, he enters into his Circle. Those who have entered into the Circle of a Master are the souls who, through their efforts, have acquired the right *(Adhikar)* of having God-realisation. When the exact moment for realisation arrives, they attain it through the Grace of the Master.

All actions in the world of duality are prompted by *sanskaras* of duality. Consciousness of duality implies the working of the impressions of duality. These impres-

Function of impressions of duality

sions of duality first serve the purpose of evolving and limiting consciousness, and then they serve the purpose of liberating it so as to facilitate Self-knowledge or God-realisation. *The soul cannot attain consciousness of its own unity unless it goes through the experiences of duality which presuppose and require corresponding impressions of duality.*

From the very beginning till the very end, the soul is subject to the momentum of impressions which constitute the destiny of the soul. These impressions are

Prarabdha Sanskaras called *Prarabdha Sanskaras. These Prarabdha Sanskaras always relate to the opposites of experience, e.g.,* the *sanskaras* of greed and its opposite, the *sanskaras* of lust and its opposite, the *sanskaras* of anger and its opposite, the *sanskaras* of bad thoughts, words and deeds and their opposites.

From the stage of the atom till the stage of the realisation of God, the soul is bound by the impressions of duality, and all that happens to it is determined by

Disappearance of sanskaras these impressions. *When the soul gets realisation of God, all its sanskaras disappear.* If it remains immersed in the experience of Divinity without coming back to normal consciousness of the world of duality, it remains eternally beyond all types of *sanskaras.* It does not have any *sanskaras* and cannot have any.

If the God-realised soul returns to normal consciousness of the world of duality, it gets a universal mind. In the universal mind with which it is endowed,

Yogayoga Sanskaras of universal mind it also gets superfluous and unbinding *sanskaras* which are known as *Yogayoga Sanskaras.* In the Beyond state the Master is eternally free from all *sanskaras,* and even when he is conscious of creation and is working in creation, he remains unbound by the *Yogayoga Sanskaras,* which sit loosely upon his universal mind. *The Yogayoga Sanskaras merely serve as channels for his universal work. They do not form a restricting chain to his consciousness.*

The *Yogayoga Sanskaras* are *automatic* in their working. All the specific contacts and links to which the Man-God responds in his working are ultimately

Function of *Yogayoga Sanskaras* based upon these *Yogayoga Sanskaras. These Yogayoga Sanskaras do not create a veil on the universal mind; they do not constitute a cloud of ignorance; they only serve as a necessary framework for the release of definitive action.* Through these *Yogayoga Sanskaras* the universal will of God is particularised in its expressions. Any action released in the world of space and time must be in relation to a certain definite situation or set of circumstances. There must always be some reason why a response is given to one situation rather than another and why it is given in one way rather than another. *The basis for the self-limitation of the actions of a soul which is in spiritual bondage, is in its Prarabdha Sanskaras, which are binding. The basis for the self-limitation of the actions of a soul which is spiritually free, is in its Yogayoga Sanskaras, which are not binding.*

If the Man-God were not to get these *Yogayoga Sanskaras* while coming down to normal consciousness, he would not be able to do any work of a definite nature.

Work of Master subject to laws of creation *The Yogayoga Sanskaras help the Man-God to particularise and materialise the Divine Will through him, and to fulfill his mission.* The Master is and knows himself to be infinite in existence, consciousness, knowledge, bliss, love and power and always remains infinite in the Beyond state. But the work he does in the world of creation is subject to the laws of creation and is therefore in one sense finite. Since his work is in relation to the unveiling of the hidden Infinity and Divinity in everyone, and since the realisation of this Infinity and Divinity is the only purpose of the entire creation, his work is *infinitely* *important;* but when it is measured by the standard of results, it has to be, like any work possible in the world, so much and no more.

But even when the work of the Man-God is measured by the magnitude of results, the results achieved by the worldly minded are mostly trivial in comparison.

Scope of Master's work determined by Yogoyoga Sanskaras

The greatest of souls who are in spiritual bondage cannot even approach the achievements of the Man-God. The Man-God has behind his work the infinite power of God, while the worldly man is working with the limited power available to him through his ego-mind. But sometimes even a Man-God achieves some limited task and then winds up his incarnation. This is not because he is limited in his power, but because *the work which is determined by his Yogayoga Sanskaras, is so much and no more. He is in no way attached to work as such.* Having finished the work given to him by his *Yogayoga Sanskaras,* he is ready to be re-absorbed in the impersonal aspect of the Infinite. He does not tarry in the world of unreality and duality a minute longer than is necessitated by his *Yogayoga Sanskaras.*

Like the Perfect Masters, the Avatar also has his Circle. When the Avatar takes an incarnation he has before him a clear-cut mission which proceeds according to a plan, and this plan is always carefully adjusted to

***Avatar* and his circle**

the flow of time. The process of the incarnation of the Avatar is unique. Before taking on the physical body and descending into the world of duality, he gives to himself and the members of his Circle special types of *sanskaras,* which are known as *Vidnyani Sanskaras.* The Circle of the Avatar always consists of one hundred and

twenty members, and all of them have to take an incarnation when the Avatar takes an incarnation. The
taking on of the *Vidnyani Sanskaras* before incarnating
in the physical body, is like the drawing of a veil upon
himself and his Circle. After taking an incarnation the
Avatar remains under this veil of *Vidnyani Sanskaras*
until the time which has been fixed by himself. When
the appointed time comes he experiences his own original divinity and begins to work through the *Vidnyani
Sanskaras,* which now have been *transmuted into the
Yogayoga Sanskaras of the Universal Mind.*

To all intents and purposes the *Vidnyani Sanskaras*
are like the ordinary *sanskaras* of duality, though they are
essentially different in nature. The *Vidnyani Sanskaras*

**Nature of *Vidnyani
Sanskaras***

prompt activities and invite
experiences which are similar
to activities and experiences
caused by ordinary *sanskaras.* But while the activities
and experiences caused by ordinary *sanskaras* have a
general tendency to strengthen the grip of illusory duality, the activities and experiences caused by *Vidnyani
Sanskaras* systematically work towards the loosening
of the grip of duality. *The logic of the working out of the
Vidnyani Sanskaras necessarily invites the realisation of
the oneness of existence. They are therefore known as a
threshold of unity.*

The members of the Circle remain under the veil
of *Vidnyani Sanskaras* until they get realisation of God
at the time fixed by the Avatar. After they get realisa-

**Fixed time for
realisation**

tion through the Avatar, the
Vidnyani Sanskaras which they
brought with them do not con-
stitute a veil, but become *Yogayoga Sanskaras,* serving
only as an instrument for the fulfillment of the divine

plan on earth.

There is an important difference between the *Vidnyani Sanskaras* and the *Yogayoga Sanskaras*. Though the *Vidnyani Sanskaras* ultimately work towards the

Difference between Vidnyani Sanskaras and Yogayoga Sanskaras

realisation of unity, they cause the experience of being limited until realisation. The *Yogayoga Sanskaras* which come after realisation do not in any way interfere with the experience of Infinity, which is above duality, although they serve as instruments for enabling and determining responses and activities in the dual world. *The working out of Vidnyani Sanskaras contributes towards one's own realisation, while the working out of Yogayoga Sanskaras contributes towards the process of realisation in others who are still in bondage.*

In the Beyond state, time, space and the whole world of phenomena are non-existent. Only in the phenomenal world of duality is there space, time or op-

Beyond state

eration of the law of cause and effect. When the Master works in the sphere of duality for the upliftment of humanity, his work becomes subject to the laws of time, space and causality. From the point of view of external work, at times he appears to be limited, though in reality he is all the time experiencing the oneness and infinity of the Beyond-state. *Though he himself is beyond time, when he works for those who are in duality, time counts.*

The Master's universal work for humanity, in general, goes on without break through the higher bodies. When he works for the members of his Circle, his action

Special working for Circle

follows a timing which he himself fixes with utmost carefulness, for it has to be a precise and definite intervention in the mechanical working out of their *sanskaras.* He works for the Circle at fixed times. Therefore those who in following the instructions received from the Master abide by the time given by him, have the benefit of his special working. From the standpoint of the special task which the Master sets before himself, time becomes an extremely important factor. The special working which the Master undertakes in relation to the members of his Circle not only touches and affects these members themselves, but also those who are closely connected with the members of his Circle.

The Circle constitutes the most important particular feature in relation to which and through which he adjusts his spiritual duty towards humanity. This par-

Master not circumscribed by Circle

ticular feature has come into existence as a result of close links and connections of several lives. Every Master has such a Circle of very close disciples, but it does not in any way create a limitation on his inward consciousness. *In his God-state the Master finds himself in the centre of the universe as well as in the centre of Everything, and there is no Circle to circumscribe his being.* In the infinity of non-duality there are no preferences. *The Circle exists only in relation to the duty and work which the Master has undertaken in the phenomenal world.* From this point of view, the Circle is as much a reality as the Himalayas.

Reincarnation and Karma

PART I
THE SIGNIFICANCE OF DEATH

THE worldly man completely identifies life with the manifestations and activities of the gross body. For him, therefore, the beginning and the end of bodily existence are also the beginning and end of the individualised soul. All his experience seems to testify to the transitoriness of the physical body, and he has often witnessed the disintegration of those physical bodies which were once vibrant with life. Hence he is naturally impelled to believe that life is conterminous with bodily existence.

Identification of soul and body

As the worldly man considers death to be the cessation of life, he gives great importance to it. There are few who contemplate on death for prolonged periods; but in spite of the fact that most persons are completely engrossed in their worldly pursuits, they are impressed by the incident of death when confronted by it.

Death as background of life

Apart from giving a general background to the scene of life, death also assumes an accentuated and overwhelming importance among the multicoloured

Importance given to death

incidents of life. Death falls among the happenings which are most dreaded and lamented, and which people, in malice or anger, try to inflict upon each other as a last penalty or worst revenge; or which they rely upon as the surest way of removing aggression or interference by others. People also invite death upon themselves in token of supreme self-sacrifice, and at times they seek it with the false hope of putting an end to all the worldly worries and problems which they are unable to face or solve. Thus, *in the minds of most persons, death assumes an accentuated and overwhelming importance.*

The overwhelming importance of death is derived from man's attachment to *particular* forms, but death loses much of its sting and importance, even for the

Persistence of life

worldly man, if he takes a broader view of the course of life. *In spite of their transitoriness, there is an unbroken continuity of life through these forms, old ones being discarded and new ones created for habitation and expression.* The recurring incident of death is matched by the recurring incident of birth. Old generations are replaced by new ones; *life is reborn in new forms, incessantly renewing and refreshing itself;* the streams of life, with their ancient origin, are ever advancing onwards through the forms which come and go like the waves of the ocean.

So, even within the limits of the experience of the worldly, there is much that should mitigate morbid thoughts of death as being an irreparable loss. *A*

Sorrow of death due to attachment

sane attitude towards death is possible only if life is considered impersonally and without any attachment to particular forms; but this the worldly man finds difficult because of his entanglement with specific forms. For him, one form is not as good as another. The form with which he identifies himself is by far the most important. The general preservation and advancement of the stream of life has for him no special interest. *What the worldly man craves is a continuation of his own form and other particular forms with which he is entangled.* His heart cannot reconcile itself to his intellect. With the vanishing of the forms which have been dear to him, he becomes a victim of unending sorrow, though life as a whole may have replaced elsewhere the lost forms with new ones.

The sorrow of death, on closer analysis, turns out to be rooted in selfishness. The person who loses his beloved may know intellectually that life as a whole

Sorrow of death a form of selfishness

has elsewhere compensated for the loss, but his only feeling is, *"What is that to me?"* When a man looks at it from his own personal point of view *death becomes a cause of unending sorrow.* From the point of view of life in general, it is an episode of minor importance.

Impersonal considerations go a long way to fortify the mind against personal sorrow caused by death, but they do not by themselves solve the wider prob-

Problems of impersonal intellect

lems which confound even the impersonal intellect of man when he considers some of the implications of death within the limits of his ordinary experience. If death is regarded as the final annihilation of individual existence, there seems to be an irreparable loss to the universe. Each individual may be in a position to give to the universe something so unique that no one else can exactly replace it. Further, there are cases of *the cutting short of an earthly career long before the attainment of perfection by the individual.* All his struggle towards the ideal, all his endeavour and enthusiasm for the great, the good and the beautiful, and all his aspiration for things divine and eternal, seem to end in the vast nothingness created by death.

The implications in assuming death to be the termination of individual existence run counter to the ineradicable expectations based upon rationalised intuition. *A*

Conflict between impure intellect and deeper intuition

conflict usually arises between the claims of intuition and the conclusion of impure intellect, which assume death to be the termination of individual existence. Such conflict is often a beginning of pure thinking, which immediately seriously challenges the usually accepted belief that death is the real termination of individual existence. Death as an extinction of life can never be wholly acceptable to the spiritual aspirations of man. Therefore belief in the immortality of the individualised soul is often accepted by the human mind without much resistance, even in the absence of direct supersensible knowledge about the existence of life after death.

Those who know from personal experience the immortality of the soul to be true, are few. *Supersensible knowledge of the existence of life after death is inaccessible to the vast majority of persons.* For them, immortality must remain an agreeable and acceptable *belief* but nothing more. It becomes a part of *personal knowledge* for those who, through scientific interest, have built up means of communication with the "other world;" or those whose special circumstances have resulted in their personally experiencing the appearance or intervention of departed spirits; or those who, through their spiritual advancement, have automatically unfolded certain latent perceptual capacities of the inner vehicles of consciousness.

Immortality of the individualised soul is rendered possible by the fact that the individualised soul is *not* the same as the physical body. The individualised soul

Material basis of immortality

continues to exist with all its *sanskaras* in the inner worlds through the medium of its mental and subtle bodies, even after it has discarded its gross body at the time of death. So, life through the medium of the gross body is only a *section* of the continuous life of the individualised soul; the other sections of its life have their expression in other worlds.

Nature is much greater than what a man can perceive through the ordinary senses of his physical body. The hidden aspects of nature consist of finer matter

Three worlds

and forces. There is no unbridgeable gulf separating the finer aspects of nature from its gross aspect. They all interpenetrate one another and exist together. The finer aspects of nature are not perceptible to ordinary man, but they are nevertheless continuous with the gross aspect which is perceptible to him. They are not remote, and yet they are inaccessible to his consciousness that is functioning through the physical senses, which are not adapted for perceiving those finer aspects of nature. Ordinary man is unconscious of the *inner planes,* just as a deaf man is unconscious of sounds, and he cannot deal with them consciously. For all practical purposes, therefore, they are other "worlds" for him. The finer and hidden part of nature has two important divisions, *viz.,* the subtle and the mental, corresponding to the subtle and mental bodies of man. The whole of nature may therefore be conveniently divided into three parts—(i) the *gross* world, (ii) the *subtle* world and (iii) the *mental* world. When the individualised soul has incarnated itself in a physical body, it expresses its life in the gross world. When it drops the outer sheath, the physical body, it continues to have its expression of life either in the subtle world through the subtle body, or in the mental world through the mental body.

Ordinarily, life in the physical body is terminated only when the *sanskaras* released for expression in that incarnation are all worked out. In some exceptional

Effects of untimely death

cases the soul has to give up its gross body before the working out of these *sanskaras* is completed. For example, the man who commits *suicide* cuts short the period of his life artificially and thereby prevents the working out of those *sanskaras* which were released for fructification. *When, due to untimely death, the sanskaras released for fructification are withheld from expression, the discarnate soul remains subject to the propelling force of these sanskaras even after the physical body has been discarded.* The momentum of the *sanskaras* which were prevented from being worked out is retained even in life after death, with the result that the departed spirit greatly desires the things of the gross world.

In such cases, the discarnate soul experiences an irresistible impulsion towards the gross world, and craves for gross objects so badly that it seeks gratifi-

Obsessions

cation of its desires through the gross body of those souls which are still incarnate. Thus the soul may want so much to drink wine that it takes to unnatural methods of gratifying the craving. It awaits its opportunity. When it finds some person drinking wine in the gross world it satisfies its own desire *through* that person by possessing his physical body. In the same way, if it wants to experience the gross manifestations of crude anger, it does so through a person in the gross world who is feeling angry. Such souls are constantly *waiting to meet and obsess some incarnate persons of similar sanskaras,* and they try to maintain their contact with the gross world through others as long as possible. *In life after death, any lingering entanglement with the gross world is a serious hindrance to the natural flow of the soul's onward life.* Those who are subject to this precarious condition must be looked upon as particularly unfortunate, since they invite upon themselves and others much unnecessary suffering by seeking unnatural gratification of coarser desires through others who are still incarnate. Compared with these unfortunate souls, the posthumous life of other souls is much smoother.

In normal cases *death occurs when all the sanskaras seeking fructification are worked out.* When the soul drops its physical body it is completely severed from

Death begins interval between two lives

all connections with the gross world, though the ego and the mind are retained with all the impressions accumulated in the earthly career. Unlike the exceptional cases of obsessing spirits, ordinary spirits try to reconcile themselves to severance from the gross world, and conform to the limitations of changed conditions and *sink into a state of subjectivity* in which a new process begins of mentally reviewing the experiences of the earthly career by reviving the *sanskaras* connected with them. Thus death inaugurates a period of comparative rest consisting in a temporary withdrawal from the gross sphere of action. *It is the beginning of an interval between the last incarnation and the next.*

Reincarnation and Karma

PART II
HELL AND HEAVEN

AFTER death there is no consciousness of the gross world since such consciousness is directly dependent on the physical body. But though the consciousness

Subjectivity of life after death

of the gross world is thus lost, the impressions of the experiences of the gross world are retained in the mental body, and they continue to express themselves through the semi-subtle sphere. During the interval between death and the next incarnation, the consciousness of the soul is turned towards these impressions resulting in a vivification of impressions and the revival of corresponding experiences. The average man does not become aware of the subtle *environment.* He is wrapped up in complete *subjectivity* and *absorbed in living through the revived impressions.*

In life after death the experiences of pain and pleasure become much more intense than they were in earthly life. *These subjective states of intensified suffer-*

Hell and heaven states of mind

ing and joy are called hell and heaven. Hell and heaven are states of mind; they should not be looked upon as being places; and though subjectively they mean a great deal to the individualised soul, they are both illusions within the greater illusion of the phenomenal world.

In the hell-state as well as in the heaven-state, desires become much more intense since they no longer require expression through the gross medium. Like desires, the experiences incurred in their fulfillment or non-fulfillment also become greatly intensified. In the earthly career

Desires and experiences intensified after dropping body

desires, as well as the pleasures and sufferings which they bring, are experienced through the medium of the gross body. The soul is of course actually using its higher bodies at the same time, but in the earthly career its consciousness is bound up with the gross body. Therefore the processes of consciousness have to pass through an additional veil which lessens their force, liveliness and intensity just as rays of light are dimmed when they are required to pass through a thick glass. *During habitation in the body, desires and experiences suffer a deterioration in intensity, but when that habitation is given up they undergo a relative increase of intensity.*

In the heaven-state the fulfillment of desires is not, as in the gross sphere, dependent upon having the object of desire. Fulfillment of desire comes merely through thinking of the object of desire. For example, if a person wishes to hear exquisite music,

Fulfillment of desires through thought

he experiences this pleasure merely by thinking about it. The imaginative idea of exquisite music becomes, in this state, a substitute for the physical sound vibrations in the gross sphere. The pleasure he derives from the thought of exquisite music is much greater than the pleasure which he derived in his earthly career from the actual hearing of physical sounds. *In the heaven-state there are no obstacles between desires and their fulfillment; the pleasure of self-fulfillment through thought or feeling is always at hand.*

In fact, even in the earthly sphere of existence some persons develop this capacity of making their pleasure independent of possession of a gross object. Beethoven,

Heaven on earth

for example, was completely deaf, and yet through the exercise of imagination alone he was able to enjoy intensely his own compositions of music. *In a sense even on earth, he might figuratively be said to have been in the heaven-state.* In the same way, a person who meditates on the Beloved with love derives happiness merely through the thought of the Beloved, without requiring the physical presence of the Beloved. After death, in the heaven-state, the enjoyment of such imaginative fulfillment is infinitely greater since consciousness is then unburdened of the outermost veil of the gross body.

Some desires have a direct relation to the possession and assimilation of gross objects through the gross body. The coarser desires of lust, gluttony or craving for

Coarser desires contribute to hell-state

drinking wine are of this type. These desires are specifically earthly because they are possessive and because they involve an element of clinging to the physical object. In these desires there is not only a preponderance of sensations derived from contact with the object, but also of those sensations which constitute the response of the body itself. These coarser desires contribute to the hell-state.

In contrast with the finer desires, the coarser desires place an infinitely heavier premium on mere sensations, quite independently of any intellectual meaning or moral

Difference between coaser and finer desires *value.* In the finer desires, such as the desire for music, there is of course an element of wanting sense contact with the physical sounds, but these sounds become important not so much in their own right, as in their capacity to express beauty. In the same way a desire to hear discourses has a hold upon the mind, not so much because of the sensations of sound, but because of the intellectual meaning and emotional appeal they convey.

Thus in the finer desires the actual sensations play a subordinate role to the derivative aspects based upon the sensations. In the coarser desires the chief element is provided by the actual sensations connected with the physical object and the sensations aroused by them through bodily response to their possession. *The organic sensations of the physical body play the greatest part in experiences connected with the coarser desires. Through them the individualised soul feels its own existence as the gross body much more effectively and vividly than through experiences connected with finer desires.*

Bodily sensations in coarser desires

Almost the entire significance of experiences brought about by the fulfillment or non-fulfillment of coarser desires is constituted by the *bodily* sensations themselves. Therefore they can rarely yield the full experience of fulfillment achieved through finer desires merely by the exercise of thought and imagination. It is characteristic of the coarser desires to insist on the possession and assimilation of the gross object itself. Any imaginative idea of the gross object

Non-fulfillment of coarser desires due to inaccesibility to gross object

merely serves the purpose of accentuating their urge to reach out to the gross object. *Since the gross object of the coarser desires is not available in the subtle world, these desires are mostly productive of intensified experience of the suffering of non-fulfillment.*

Just as in this world the presence of coarser desires leads to the preponderance of suffering over pleasure, so in the life after death the revived experiences con-

Sufferings of hell and the pleasures of heaven

nected with these coarser desires leads to a *preponderance of suffering over pleasure,* thus bringing into existence the *hell-state.* Similarly, in the life after death the revived experiences connected with the finer desires lead to a *preponderance of pleasure over suffering,* thus bringing into existence the *heaven-state.*

But hell and heaven are both states of bondage *subject to the limitations of the opposites* of pleasure and pain. Both are states whose duration is determined by

Time in subtle world

the nature, amount and intensity of the accumulated impressions. *Time in the subtle world is not the same as time in the gross world due to the increased subjectivity of the states of consciousness;* but though time in the subtle world is thus *incommensurable* with time in the gross world, it is strictly determined by the impressions accumulated in the gross world. However, the important fact is that the hell-state and the heaven-state are far from being lasting, and after they have served their purpose in the life of the individualised soul they both come to an end.

The coarser sensual desires like lust, and their emotional products like hate and anger, all contribute to the life of delusion and suffering prevalent in the

Vivication of impressions

hell-state. The finer desires like idealistic aspirations, aesthetic and scientific interests, good-will towards neighbours and others, and their emotional products like personal love or fellow-feeling, contribute to the life of enlightenment and pleasure prevalent in the heaven-state. *These states for most persons consist in reliving the experiences of the earthly life by vivification of the impressions left by them.* Their duration and nature are dependent upon the duration and nature of the experiences undergone by the person in his physical body.

Just as the gramophone record is set aside after the needle of the sound-arm has travelled through each groove, *so the hell-state and the heaven-state terminate af-*

Termination of hell and heaven

ter consciousness has traversed the imprints left by earthly life. Just as the song produced by the gramophone record is strictly determined by the original song which has been recorded on it, so the quality of intensified and magnified experiences through which the soul passes after death is strictly determined by the kind of life which the person led on earth in the physical body. From this point of view, heaven and hell are shadows cast by man's earthly life.

Heaven and hell would, however, serve no specially useful purpose in the life of the individual soul if they were to consist *merely* of mental revival of the

Retrospective survey of earthly experiences

earthly past. That would mean bare repetition of what has already occurred. Consciousness in these after-death states is in a position to make a *leisurely and effective survey of the animated record of earthly life.* Through intensification of experiences it can observe their nature with better facility and results. On earth, the consciousness of most persons is *predominantly objective and forward-looking* and under the pressure of unspent *sanskaras.* It is mostly concerned with the possible fulfillment of *sanskaras* through the *present* or the *future.* In life after death the consciousness of most persons is *predominantly subjective and retrospective.* In the absence of forward-goading *sanskaras* it is, as in reminiscences, mostly preoccupied with reviewing and assessing the significance of the *past.*

The fret and fury of immediate responses to the changing situations of earthly life is replaced in life after death by a more leisurely mood freed from the urgency of immediately needed actions.

Analogy of cinema

All the experience of the earthly career is now available for reflection in a form more vivid than is possible through memory in earthly life. *The snapshots of earthly life have all been taken on the cinematic film of the mind and it is now time to study the original earthly life through the magnified projections of the filmed record on the screen of subjectivised consciousness.*

Thus the hell-state and the heaven-state become instrumental in the *assimilation of experience* acquired in the earthly phase, so that the individualised soul can start its next incarnation in the physical body with all the advantage of digested experience.

Assimilation of earthly experiences

The lessons learned by the soul through much stock-taking and reflection are confirmed on the mind-body by the power of their magnified suffering or happiness. They become, for the next incarnation, part and parcel of the intuitive make-up of active consciousness, without in any way involving detailed revival of the individual events of the previous incarnation. The truths absorbed by the mind in the life after death become in the next incarnation a part of the inborn wisdom. *Developed intuition is consolidated and compressed understanding distilled through a multitude of diverse experiences gathered in previous lives.*

Different souls start with different degrees of intuitive wisdom as their initial capital for the experiments and adventures of their earthly career. This intuition

Contribution of hell and heaven to release of intuitive wisdom

may seem to have been the product of past experiences, thus adding to the equipment of the psyche, but it is more truly an unfoldment of what was already latent in the individualised soul. From this deeper point of view *the experiences of earthly life as well as the reflective and consolidatory processes to which they are subjected in life after death are merely instrumental in gradually releasing to the surface the intuitive wisdom which is already latent in the soul from the very beginning of creation.* As is true of the earthly career and its experiences, the states of hell and heaven in the life after death are also integral parts of and incidents in that journey of the individualised soul which is ultimately meant to reach the source of all things.

Reincarnation and Karma

THOSE who have immediate access to the supersensible truths concerning the life of the soul and its reincarnation know, through their unclouded perception, that so-called birth is only an incarnation of the individualised soul in the gross sphere.

Incidents of birth and death

The unbroken continuity of the life of the reincarnating soul is punctuated by birth and death, both of which are comparable to gateways in the stream of life as it advances from one type of existence to another. Both are equally necessary in the greater life of the soul, and the interval between death and birth is as necessary as the interval between birth and death.

As is true of those who consider death to be the termination of individual existence, so those who consider the birth of a body to be its beginning are also confronted with a conflict between their false assumptions and the claims of rationalised intuition. From the standpoint of individual justice, the uneven distribution of good and bad in relation to material happiness or prosperity

Demands of intuition

seems seriously to impugn the rationality and justification of the entire scheme of the universe. To see the
virtuous at times suffering deeply and the vicious possessing the amenities of pleasure, creates insurmountable difficulties for anyone who prefers to look upon life
as being meant to fulfill an eternal and divine purpose.

Unless there is some deeper explanation forthcom-
ing, the human mind is riddled with agonising perplexi-
ties that tend to embitter a man's general outlook on
Tendency to accept
deeper explanations
life and foster a callous cyni-
cism which, in many ways, is
even worse than the deepest
personal sorrow which death may cause. But in spite of
all appearances to the contrary, the human mind has in
it *an inborn tendency to try to restore to itself a deep and
unshakable faith in the intrinsic sanity and value of life.*
Except where artificial resistances are created, it finds
acceptable those explanations which are in conformity
with this deeper law of the spirit.

Those who have direct access to the truth of reincarnation are even fewer than those who have direct
access to the truth of the immortality of the individual
Effect of changing
brain
soul. The memories of all past
lives are stored and preserved
in the mind-body of the in-
dividual soul, but they are not accessible to the consciousness of ordinary persons because a veil is drawn
over them. When the soul changes its physical body it
gets a new brain, and its normal waking consciousness
functions in close association with the brain processes.
Under ordinary circumstances, only the memories of
the present life can appear in consciousness because
*the new brain acts as a hindrance to the release of the
memories of those experiences which had to be gathered*

through the medium of other brains in past lives.

In rare cases, in spite of the resistance offered by the brain, some memories of past lives leak into the present life in the form of dreams which are completely

Memory of past lives

unexplainable in terms of the present life. A man may see persons in his dreams whom he has never seen in his present life. It often happens that the persons who appeared in the dreams were persons whom he had met in his past lives. But of course such dreams, when they are of the ordinary type, cannot be treated as a *memory* of past lives. They merely indicate that the imagination which worked in dreams was influenced by materials taken from the past lives of the man. *The real memory of past lives is clear, steady and sure like the memory of the present life.* When it comes to a man, he no longer has any doubt about his having existed in several lives along with many others. Just as he cannot doubt his own past life in the present incarnation, he cannot doubt his life in his past incarnations.

The number of persons who can remember their past lives is very small compared with the vast majority, who are so completely bound to the gross sphere of

Release of memory of past lives

existence that they do not even suspect supersensible realities. The release of such memories is severely conditioned by the limitations of the brain, as long as consciousness is entangled with the physical body and its brain processes. *When consciousness is emancipated from the limitations imposed by the brain, it can recover and re-establish the memories of past lives which are all stored in the mental body.* This involves a degree of *detachment and understanding* which only the spiritually advanced persons can have. The memory of past lives can come with full clarity and certainty, even to those who are still crossing the inner planes but have not yet become spiritually perfect.

The memory of past lives does not come back to a person, except in abnormal and rare cases, unless he is sufficiently advanced from the spiritual point of view. This provision made by the laws of life secures unhampered spiritual evolution of the individualised soul. At first view it might seem that loss of memory of previous lives is all a loss, but this is far from being so. *For most purposes, knowledge about past lives is not at all necessary for the guidance of the onward course of spiritual evolution. Spiritual evolution consists in guiding life in the light of the highest values perceived through intuition, and not in allowing it to be determined by the past.* In many cases, even the memory of the present life acts as an obstacle for certain adjustments demanded by the spiritual requirements of the changing situations of life. The problem of emancipation may, in a sense, be said to be a problem of securing freedom from the past which, in the case of those who are bound to the wheel of birth and death, inexorably shapes the present life.

Loss of memory of past lives does not affect progress

Life would be infinitely more complicated if one who is not spiritually advanced were burdened by the conscious memory of numberless past lives. He would be dazed and unsettled by the diversity of settings in which persons would appear to him in the light of his memory. He is not called upon to face such confusion, however, because he is shielded from the resurrection of the memory of past lives. Things and persons come to him in a limited and definite context

Shielding from complications

and setting, with the result that he finds it easy to determine his actions and responses in the light of what he knows from the present life. This does not mean that his actions and responses are *entirely* determined by what he knows from his present life. All that has happened in past lives also has its own unconscious but effective share in determining his actions and responses. But in spite of the actual influence of the past lives, the fact remains that *since he is shielded from the resurrection of conscious memory, his consciousness is not subject to the confusion which would result if the conscious memory of past lives were to be among the data which he had to consider for the purpose of determining his actions and responses.*

The resurrection of the memory of past lives can be faced without confusion or loss of balance only when the person has become desireless and has lost all feeling of "mine" and "thine." The

Condition of safety in release of memory

persons whom he has once looked upon as belonging to him might be seen in the present life belonging to someone else, and if he were to continue his attachments and supposed claims he would create untold complications, misery and confusion for himself and others. *Possessiveness of all types has to be purged from the mind if the aspirant is to be spiritually prepared to withstand the disturbing influence of memory from past lives.*

When a man is spiritually prepared he is completely desireless and full of impersonal love. All entanglements of the personal ego have disappeared from

Spiritual preparation

his mind. *He can look upon his old friends and enemies with the same equanimity.* He is so lifted out of his limitations that he is the same to relations and non-relations

from his past and present lives. He is free from the idea
of any pressing claims and counter-claims on his part
against others, or of others against himself, because he
has realised the deeper truth of the unity of all life and
the illusoriness of mundane happenings.

It is only when a person is thus spiritually prepared
that he is unaffected by the revived memory of past
lives. Only then is it worthwhile for him to have access

**Wise use of resur-
rected memory**

to it, for he can then have that
cool and unerring judgment
and pure, incorruptible love
which enable him to make right and wise use of the new
knowledge gathered through the resurrected memory
of past lives. This knowledge opens to him a great deal
of information about his own incarnations and those
of others connected with him in past lives. *It not only
enables him to advance further on the path by conscious
karmic adjustments,* but also to help others on the path
by directing them in the light of their past lives.

The speed of spiritual evolution is faster after the
natural recovery of the memory of past incarnations.
Disentanglement from mundane things is facilitated

**Advantages of recov-
ered memory**

by conscious knowledge of the
history of the development of
such entanglements. Evolution
which was mostly unconscious of the limiting past, now
becomes conscious of it. *The obstacles as well as the
facilities created by the past are now in the reach of consciousness and therefore are capable of intelligent and
careful handling.* Inarticulate intuition is supplemented
by rationalised data. Therefore action has less possibility of error and becomes more potent in producing
desirable results.

The Masters of Wisdom, having become spiritually

perfect, have no special interest in past incarnations. They are among the many unimportant facts of mun-

Shortcut through knowledge of past lives

dane existence. If they make any use of their knowledge of the past lives of a person, it is only to help him on towards the eternal Truth. Their knowledge of the past places them in a special position to give an aspirant just that guidance which he needs. The details of the Path are often determined by (i) the incidents of the past, (ii) the manner in which the aspirant has sought the highest Truth in his past lives and (iii) the obstacles or facilities which he has created for himself through his past doings. All these things, which are hidden from the aspirant, are open to the unclouded perception of the Master who uses his knowledge in order to accelerate the spiritual progress of the seeker of the Truth. The Master leads the aspirant from the place in which he has landed himself through the experimentation and search of several lives. *In spiritual matters, as in mundane matters, greater and unerring knowledge means economy of energy and time.*

Reincarnation and Karma

THE individualised soul has its beginning and source in the infinite, formless, sexless and indivisible being of God, Who is beyond all forms of duality or evolution. *With the beginning of the individualised soul there is the beginning of duality and evolution, though the specific form of duality consisting in the distinction and attraction based upon sex makes its appearance at a later stage of evolution.* Duality exists as soon as there is subject and object—a centre of consciousness (howsoever dim) and its environment. Sex, however, is a specific kind of *bodily attraction* which presupposes differentiation of forms, a specific kind of psychic entanglement with the forms, and specific expression of life and energy.

Sex a specific form of duality

In the mineral kingdom there is no sex. In the kingdom of plants and trees the bodily differentiations of sex, with specialised biological functions, have come into existence. Plants and trees do not generate *sex-consciousness,* since the development of

Sex in minerals and plants

consciousness in plants and trees is rudimentary and its expressions are not influenced by these bodily differentiations. Contact between the male and the female in plants and trees is (due to their being fixed in the ground) *not direct,* but only *indirect,* through the intermediate agency of winds, bees, etc. Therefore, while from the standpoint of evolution of *forms* sex-differentiation may be said to have begun to emerge even at the level of plants and trees, from the point of view of their own *consciousness* they cannot be said to have any sex because *their consciousness of duality is not in any way coloured by sex.*

In the evolution of sex-duality, plants and trees stand midway between minerals which have no sex, and birds and animals which have it in its complete form. Just

Sex in birds and animals

before the soul incarnates in human form, it arrives at full consciousness and energy in the last animal forms. It then drops the animal body to take a human body. *Reincarnation of the individualised soul through human forms is preceded by its successive incarnations in the sub-human forms.*

In animals, sex not only expresses itself through the bodily differences and activities, but is a deep-rooted factor which affects consciousness. Since humans

Psyche modified by sex

inherit their bodies as well as consciousness from highly evolved animals like apes, the humans also find themselves subject to sex-duality. *In humans sex is so completely developed that it is no longer a matter merely of the body. It substantially modifies the psyche* and seeks its expression through the body in accordance with whether the form is male or female.

After attaining the human form, as a rule there

is *no reversion to animal forms;* the case of retrogression to sub-human forms comes under special and rare

Male and female incarnations

exceptions. For the soul which has once attained human status, the normal course is to go through countless reincarnations in the human form itself. The human form may sometimes be male and sometimes female according to the *sanskaras* and the spiritual requirements of the soul.

The female form has the special prerogative that even the Sadgurus and the Avatars have to be born through the female form. The male form has the pre-

Prerogatives of male and female forms

rogative that the majority of the Sadgurus appear in male form. Women can become saints and Sadgurus, but the Avatar always appears in male form.

The general aids and handicaps of an incarnation are always determined by the specific *sanskaras* which the individual soul has accumulated in the past. *The*

Facilities and handicaps of incarnation determined by accumulated *sanskaras*

needs involved in the further development of the soul are related to the nature of its accumulated sanskaras. Therefore these accumulated sanskaras really determine whether the soul takes its incarnation on the earth in the East or in the West, or in the male form or in the female form, or in one cycle of existence or another. The facilities afforded by a specific incarnation are dependent not only upon whether an incarnation is in the male form or female form, but also upon whether it takes place in one cycle of existence or another cycle of existence, and whether it matches the tenor of earthly life in the eastern hemisphere or in the western hemisphere.

Roughly speaking, today on the whole the East has developed more on spiritual lines than on material lines, with the result that the Eastern mind has a spontaneous

East and West

aspiration for God. The West on the whole has developed more on material lines than on spiritual lines, with the result that the Western mind has a spontaneous urge towards intellectual and artistic things. An incarnation in the East usually brings with it a greater tendency towards spiritual life than an incarnation in the West, and an incarnation in the West usually brings with it a greater tendency towards material life than an incarnation in the East. But *the soul has to experience the material as well as the spiritual aspects of life before it is freed from the fetters of divided life.* Therefore the same soul has to incarnate in the East as well as in the West.

If a soul has had many successive incarnations in the East and then takes an incarnation in the West, it carries with it the impressions of its lives in the East

Change of sphere

and, though living in the West, it leads a life essentially in conformity with the Eastern pattern. If a soul has made many successive incarnations in the West and then takes an incarnation in the East, it carries with it the impressions of its lives in the West and, though living in the East, it leads a life which is in conformity with the Western pattern. Sometimes we therefore have a *European soul in an Indian form or an Indian soul in European form.* It must be borne in mind that this distinction is only relative to past incarnations and *sanskaras,* and that the soul as such is beyond such distinctions.

The facilities afforded by male and female incarnations respectively are not rigidly invariable. They change according to the cycles of existence as well as whether

Cycles of existence

the incarnation is in the East or in the West. In some ages men are more active, energetic and materially-minded than women. In other ages, the reverse is true. In the past the women of the East were brave and intellectual. They considered no sacrifice too great for the happiness and well-being of their husbands, and their spiritual humility extended to looking upon the husband as God Himself. Now in the Eastern hemisphere the average man has greater spiritual inclination than the average woman, just as in the West the average woman of today has greater spiritual inclination than the average man. A man living in the East is different from a man living in the West, and a woman living in the East is different from a woman living in the West. The joke is that in comparison with members of the opposite sex, the *same* soul shows varying degrees of superiority, inferiority or equality with regard to spiritual or material matters, depending upon the cycle of existence, the sex of its body and the earthly sphere in which it takes an incarnation.

Reincarnation and Karma

PART V
THE NEED FOR MALE AND FEMALE INCARNATIONS

THOUGH the facilities afforded by each sex vary according to the age and place in which the incarnation occurs, nevertheless *each sex affords special facilities for the development of experience along specific lines.*

Facilities of male and female forms

The lessons readily learned in male incarnations may not be easily attainable through female incarnations, and the lessons readily learned in female incarnations may not be easily attainable in male incarnations. *As a rule, men excel in qualities of the head and will. They are capable of sound judgment and steadfast purpose. As a rule, women excel in qualities of the heart.* They are capable of intense love which makes them welcome any sacrifice for the loved one. It is due to this capacity of women for love that, in devotional references, the name of the female has invariable precedence, as when the *Bhaktas* sing of Radha-Krishna or Sita-Ram. In qualities of the heart women are usually superior to men, and in qualities of the head and will men are usually superior to women. The interesting point is that the same soul excels in the qualities of the

heart, or in the qualities of the head and will, according to whether it takes an incarnation in a female or
male form. *The alternate development of specific spiritual
qualities goes on through the alternation between the male
and female forms, until the development is all-sided.*

Since male and female incarnations are equally
necessary for self-knowledge, it is not right to look upon
one as being more important than the other. Though

**Male and female
incarnations equally
necessary**

there are differences between
the nature of the respective facilities afforded by them, they
are both indispensable. *The
soul must go through male incarnations as well as female
incarnations if it is to have that richness of experience
which is a condition of attaining the realisation that the
soul, in itself, is beyond all forms of duality, including the
accentuated duality based on sex.*

Before the soul is set free from all *sanskaras* it
assumes numerous male forms and numerous female
forms. If the soul were to incarnate only in the male

**Male and female
incarnations supple-
ment each other**

forms or only in the female
forms, its experience would
remain one-sided and incomplete. The duality of experience
can be overcome only through understanding, and the
understanding of experience is only partial as long as it
moves within the limits of only one of the two opposites.
*Unity of the subject and object of experience is unattain-
able as long as there is in the object any aspect or element
which is not fully covered by one's own experience, and
this applies particularly to sex-duality.*

*The psyche of the soul retains the gathered experience
of male and female incarnations. Since the soul identifies
itself with the body, the psychological tendencies which*

Division of psyche

harmonise with the sex of the body find a suitable medium for expression. *The psychological tendencies which are characteristic of the opposite sex are ordinarily suppressed into the unconscious part of the psyche, because they do not harmonise with the sex of the body and find the medium of expression obstructive.* When the soul takes a female body the male tendencies are, so to speak, held in abeyance and only the female tendencies are released for expression. In the same way, when the soul takes a male body the female tendencies are held in abeyance and the male tendencies are released for expression.

Identification with the body involves identification with the sex of the body. It therefore implies a free play only for that limited part of the psyche which is in tune with the sex of the body. Since the other part of the psyche is repressed and latent in the un-

Genesis of sex-entanglement

conscious, there arises in the conscious part a feeling of incompleteness as well as a tendency to restore completeness through attachment to persons of the opposite sex. *By getting entangled with the opposite sex the buried part of the psyche which did not go well with the body seeks some kind of expression through another. From this point of view sex-attraction might be said to be a result of the effort which the mind makes to unite with its own unconscious part.*

Sex is a manifestation of the ignorant attempt which the conscious mind makes to compensate for the psychic fragmentation entailed by identification with the sex of the body. *This attempt to compensate for fragmentation is doomed to be futile, however,*

Self-defeating compensation

because it is not only based upon identification with the

body, but actually accentuates it by setting into opposition the body of the opposite sex and getting entangled with it through attachment and possessiveness.

When the soul is trying to overcome sex-duality through detachment towards the opposite sex, it is paving a way for understanding the experience asso-

Understanding through detachment

ciated with the opposite sex from *within*. Then a man tries to understand a woman, not through the eyes of the male, but through the imaginative reaching out towards what the woman feels herself to be in her own personal experience. In the same way, a woman tries to understand a man, not through the eyes of the female, but through the imaginative reaching out towards what a man feels himself to be in his own personal experience. So, paradoxical though it may seem, the *form* of the opposite sex prevents the true understanding of *experience* associated with the opposite sex. *Detachment from the form of the opposite sex facilitates true understanding of the experience associated with the opposite sex, because it removes the barrier created by sex-obsessed imagination.*

If a man is transcending sex-duality and trying to understand the experience associated with the opposite sex, sometimes he actually exhibits the psychological

Freedom from sex-ridden imagination

traits usually associated with the opposite sex. Thus some aspirants in the male body at one phase or another actually put on the clothes of females, talk like them, feel like them and take on their psychic traits and habits. But this is only a passing phase. When inner understanding of the relevant experiences is complete, they neither experience themselves as male alone nor as female alone, *but as being beyond the distinction of sex.* The experiences connected with the male and female forms are both accessible and intelligible to the aspirant who has transcended sex-distinction. He remains unaffected by the limitations of either because, through understanding, *he has freed himself from the limiting obsessions characteristic of sex-ridden imagination.*

The completeness which the mind seeks is not attainable through attachment to other forms and their accession. It is to be sought *within* by recapturing the lost unity of the mind.

Reconciliation of conscious and unconscious mind

Reconciliation of the conscious and the unconscious mind is possible not through sex-attraction or through other forms of possessiveness, but through non-identification with the body and its sex. Non-identification with the body removes the barrier which prevents the amalgamation and integration of the total experiences deposited in the psyche of the soul. Completeness within is to be sought by overcoming sex-duality and distinction which accentuates identification with the body.

To be free from attachment to the opposite sex is to be free from domination of sex of the body in which the soul has incarnated itself, thereby annihilating the

Divine love

majority of those *sanskaras* which compel the soul to identify itself with the body. The transcending of sex-duality does not itself amount to the overcoming of all duality, but it certainly goes a long way towards facilitating the complete transcendence of duality in all its forms. On the other hand, it is equally true that *the problem of sex-duality is a part of the problem of duality as such. Its complete solution comes when the wider problem of all duality is solved through Divine Love in which there is neither "I" nor "you," neither man nor woman.* The purpose of male and female incarnations is the same as the purpose of evolution itself; it is to enable man to arrive at his own undivided and indivisible existence.

Reincarnation and Karma

PART VI
THE OPERATION OF KARMA
THROUGH SUCCESSIVE LIVES

IN the successive incarnations of an individual soul, there is not only a thread of continuity and identity (manifested in personal memory and revived in the case of advanced souls), but there

Incarnations governed by law of *Karma*

is also an uninterrupted reign of the law of cause and effect through the persistence and operation of *Karma*. The successive incarnations with all their particulars are closely and unfailingly determined by rational law, so that it becomes possible for the individual soul to mould its future through wise and intelligent action. The actions of past lives determine the conditions and circumstances of the present life, and the actions of the present life have their share in determining the conditions and circumstances of future lives. *Successive incarnations of the individual soul yield their full significance only in the light of the operation of the law of Karma.*

The intermittent incarnations in the gross world are only apparently disconnected. *Karma persists as a connecting link and determining factor through the mental body, which remains a permanent and constant fac-*

Persistence of *Karma* through mental body   *tor through all the lives of the soul.* The law of *Karma* and its manner of operation cannot be fully intelligible as long as the gross body and the gross world are considered to be the only facts of existence. *Karmic* determination is made possible by the existence of subtle and mental bodies and worlds.

The place in which one can possess physical consciousness is the gross world. The planes on which one can possess consciousness of desires are in the subtle

Mental and subtle bodies   world, and the planes on which the soul can have mental consciousness are in the mental world. The source of desire is to be found in the mind, which is on the mental planes. Here the seed of desire is attached to the mind; the desire exists here in an involved form, in the same way as the tree is latent in the seed. The mental body, which is the seat of the mind, is often called *Karana Sharira* or the causal body *because it stores within itself the seeds or the causes of all desires.* The mind retains all impressions and dispositions in a latent form. The limited "I" or ego is composed of these *sanskaras.* However, the actual manifestation of *sanskaras* in consciousness, as expressed through different mental processes, takes place in the subtle body.

The soul, which in reality is one and undifferentiated, is apparently individualised through the limitations of the mental body which is the seat of the ego-mind.

Formation and continuation of ego-mind   The ego-mind is formed by the accumulated impressions of past experiences and actions; and it is this ego-mind which constitutes the kernel of the existence of the reincarnating individual. The ego-mind, as a reservoir of latent impressions, is the state of the mental body. The ego-mind, becoming spirit and experiencing activated and manifested impressions, is the state of the subtle body. The ego-mind, as descended in the gross sphere for creative action, is the state of a physical incarnation. Thus *the ego-mind, which is seated in the mental body, is the entity which has all the phases of continued existence as a separate individual.*

The ego-mind, seated in the mental body, takes lower bodies according to the impressions stored in it. These impressions determine whether a person will die young or old, whether he will experience health or illness or both, whether he will be beautiful or ugly, whether he will suffer

Impressions in ego-mind determine conditions of incarnation

from physical handicaps like blindness or will enjoy general efficiency of the body, whether he will have a sharp or a dull intellect, whether he will be pure or impure of heart, fickle or steadfast in will and whether he will be immersed in the pursuit of material gains or will seek the inner light of the spirit.

The ego-mind in its turn becomes modified through the deposited impressions of *Karma* (which include not only gross and physical action, but thought and feeling),

Game of duality

and *the circumstances of each incarnation are adjusted to the composition and needs of the ego-mind.* Thus if a person has developed certain special capacities or tendencies in one incarnation, he takes them on to the succeeding incarnations; and things that have been left incomplete in one incarnation can be completed in the incarnations which follow. Through the persistence of impressions, the *Karmic* links which have been forged in one incarnation are carried on and developed in succeeding incarnations. Thus *those who have been closely associated with each other through good or bad dealings, tend to have recurring contacts, carrying on the game of duality* far enough to gather so much experience of the opposites that the soul, out of the fullness of its experience, eventually becomes ripe for dropping the ego-mind and turning inwards to know itself as the Oversoul.

If there has been a give and take between certain persons that forges *Karmic* and *sanskaric* ties between them and creates *claims and counter-claims,* they have

Claims and counter-claims created by give and take

to come together and carry on fresh deals in order to meet these claims and counter-claims. *That which a person gives with a selfish motive binds him in the same way as that which he takes with a sense of separateness.* The deal of give or take, which thus binds, need not be purely on a material plane in the form of exchange of goods or money, or in the performing of some physical tasks. It could consist of exchange of views or feelings.

If a person pays respect to a saint on the higher planes he creates a claim against him so that even if the saint himself is crossing the inner planes and treading

Karma of interference

the Path, he has to tarry and give such help as will bring the person paying respect to that point on the Path which he himself has reached. Paying respect to a saint thus amounts to *Karma of interference.* Though respect, as such, is a good thing to receive, in receiving it the saint may have to halt on the Path until he has helped the person who came to him and gave him respect.

The quick and unfailing responsiveness of souls is expressed in the law that hate begets hate, lust begets lust and love begets love. This law operates not only during a single life-time but *across several lives.* A man feels impelled to hate or fear an enemy of past lives, although present life may not have provided him with any apparent reason for this attitude. In the same way, without any apparent reason from the present life, he is impelled to love and help a friend of past lives. In most cases the person may not be aware of the reason for his unaccountable attitude, but that does not mean there is no reason for it. Many things which seem inexplicable on the surface, become intelligible when considered in the light of *Karmic* links brought forward from past lives.

Responsiveness of souls

The law of Karma is law exhibiting itself through continuously changing mutual adjustments, which must go on where there are several individual souls who seek self-expression in a common world. It is an outcome of the responsiveness of ego-minds. The rhythm in which two souls start their relationship tends to perpetuate itself unless the soul, through fresh intelligent *Karma,* changes the rhythm and raises it to a higher quality.

Law of *karma* is law of action and reaction

As a rule, accumulated *Karma* has a certain inertia of its own. It does not change the nature of its momentum unless there is a special reason for it. *Before Karma is created the individual has a sort of freedom to choose what it shall be; but after it has been delineated it becomes a factor which cannot be ignored and which either has to be expended through the results which it invites, or counteracted by fresh and appropriate Karma.*

Freedom of *Karma*

The pleasure and pain experienced in life on earth,

the success or failure which attend it, the attainments
and obstacles with which it is strewn, the friends and

Fate   foes who appear in it, all are
determined by the *Karma* of
past lives. *Karmic determination is popularly designated
as fate.* Fate, however, is not some foreign and oppres-
sive principle. *Fate is man's own creation pursuing him
from past lives;* and just as it has been shaped by past
Karma, it can also be modified, remoulded and even
undone through *Karma* in the present life.

If the nature of the *Karma* in earthly life is determined by impressions stored in the ego-mind, they in
turn are determined by the nature of *Karma* in earthly

**Creative *karma*
possible only in
physical body**   life. The impressions in the ego-
mind and the nature of *Karma*
are interdependent. The *Karma*
on earth plays an important
part in shaping and reshaping the impressions in the
ego-mind, and giving it a momentum which decides the
further destiny of the individual. *It is in the arena of
earthly existence that creative and effective Karma can
express through the medium of the gross body.*

Proper understanding and use of the law of *Karma*
enables man to become *master of his own destiny*
through intelligent and wise action. Each person has

**Becoming master of
destiny**   become what he is through his
own accumulated actions; and
it is through his own actions
that he can mould himself according to the pattern of
his heart, or finally emancipate himself from the reign
of *Karmic* determination which governs him through
life and death.

Broadly speaking, *Karma* is of two kinds: that
which binds and that which helps towards emancipation

and Self-realisation. Good as well as bad *Karma* binds as

Unbinding *Karma*

long as it springs from the ego-mind and feeds it, but *Karma becomes a power for emancipation when it springs from right understanding.* Right understanding in this respect is best imparted by the Masters who know the soul in its true nature and destiny, along with the complications created by *Karmic* laws.

The *Karma* which truly counts comes into existence after the person has developed a sense of distinction between good and bad. During the first seven

Karma begins with distinction between good and bad

years of childhood the impressions which are released for expression are very faint. They also entail a consciousness of the world which is correspondingly less responsive to the distinctions of the world. Therefore the actions of children under seven years do not leave any strong or effective impressions on the ego-mind, and they do not play any important part in shaping their future. *True and effective Karma, which moulds the ego-mind and its future, begins after the soul develops a sense of responsibility.* This sense of responsibility is dependent upon a sense of *distinction between good and bad* which usually dawns fully when the soul has spent the first few years of childhood.

The law of *Karma* is, in the world of values, the *counterpart of the law of cause and effect* which operates in the physical world. If there were no law of cause

Comparison with law of cause aned effect

and effect in the physical world there would be chaos, and people would not know which thing might be expected to follow which thing. In the same way, if there were no law of *Karma* in the world of values, there would be an utter uncertainty of results in the world of values which men cherish, and people would not know whether to expect good or bad results from their actions. In the world of physical events there is a law of *conservation of energy* according to which no energy is ever lost. In the world of values there is a law that *once Karma comes into existence, it does not mysteriously flitter away without leading to its natural result, but persists until it bears its own fruit or is undone through counter-Karma.* Good actions lead to good results, and bad actions lead to bad results.

The moral order of the universe is sustained through the systematic connection between cause and effect in the world of values. If the law of *Karma* were subject to any

Law of *Karma* maintains moral order of universe

relaxation, reversals or exceptions, and if not strictly applicable in the domain of values, there would be no moral order in the universe, and human existence would be precarious from the viewpoint of attainment of values. In a universe without moral order, human endeavour would be perpetually fraught with doubt and uncertainty. *There cannot be any serious pursuit of values if there is no assured connection between means and ends and if the law of Karma can be set aside.* The inflexibility of the law of *Karma* is a condition for significant human action which would be utterly impossible if the law of *Karma* could be safely ignored or flouted.

In its inviolability the law of *Karma* is like the other laws of nature. *However, the rigorousness of the operation of Karmic laws does not come to the soul as the oppres-*

Karma and responsibility

siveness of some external and blind power, but as something involved in the rationality of the scheme of life. Karmic determination is the condition of true responsibility. It means that a man will reap as he sows. What a person gathers by way of experience is invariably connected with what he does.

If a person has done an evil turn to someone he must accept the penalty for it and welcome the *evil rebounding upon himself.* If he has done a good turn to

Law of *Karma* an expression of justice

someone he must also receive the reward for it and enjoy the *good rebounding upon himself. What he does for another he has also done for himself, although it may take time for him to realise that this is exactly so. The law of Karma might be said to be an expression of justice or a reflection of the unity of life in the world of duality.*

Reincarnation and Karma

PART VII
THE DESTINY OF THE
REINCARNATING INDIVIDUAL

THE series of incarnations which the soul is impelled to take through *Karmic* determination, has a tendency to become endless. Through innumerable lives

Karmic debts and dues

the aspirant has come into contact with countless persons, and he has had all kinds of dealings of give and take with them. He is entangled in a web consisting of all sorts of debts to pay and dues to recover. According to *Karmic* law *he can avoid neither the debts nor the dues, since both are the outcome of Karma inspired by desire.* He keeps incarnating in order to pay off his debts and to recover his dues, but even when he means to clear up the account he is often unable to do so.

All persons with whom a man has *Karmic* links of debts or dues may not be incarnate when he has taken a body. Or, owing to the limitations imposed by his own

Difficulty clearing up debts and dues

capacities and circumstances, he may be unable to meet all the complex requirements of the situation. When he is trying to clear up accounts with those with whom he has past links, in this very attempt he cannot help *creating fresh claims and counterclaims* concerning them. Even with new persons he cannot help but create debts and dues of diverse kinds and magnitudes, and get involved with them. *A man goes on adding to his debts and dues with the result that there is no getting out of his endlessly increasing and complex Karmic entanglements.*

The spinning of the yarn of *Karmic* debts and dues would be endless if there had been no provision for getting out of the Karmic entanglements through the help of the Master. He can not only

Master can assist clearing debts and dues

initiate the aspirant into the supreme art of unbinding *Karma,* but can become directly instrumental in freeing him from his *Karmic* entanglements. *The Master has attained unity with God, Whose cosmic and universal life includes all persons. Being one with all life, he can become, in his representative capacity for the sake of the aspirant, the medium for the clearing up of all debts and dues which have come into existence through the aspirant's dealings with countless persons contacted in his incarnations.* If a person must get bound to someone, it is best for him to get bound to God or the Master, because this tie ultimately facilitates emancipation from all other *Karmic* ties.

When the good *Karma* of past lives has secured for the aspirant the benefit of having a Master, the best thing that he can do is to surrender himself to the Master and to serve him.

Relation between Master and disiciple carried on through several lives

Through surrenderance the aspirant throws the burden of his *Karma* on the Master who has to think out ways and means

of freeing him from it. Through serving the Master he
wins an opportunity to get clear of his *Karmic* entanglements. The relation between the Master and the disciple
is often carried on from one life to another for several
reincarnations. Those who have been connected with
the Master in past lives are drawn to him by an unconscious magnetism, not knowing why they are thus
drawn. There is usually a long history to the apparently
unaccountable devotion which the disciple feels for his
Master. The disciple is often beginning where he had left
off in the last incarnation.

When the disciple invites the attention and grace
of a Master it is not without reason. Sometimes the
Master seems to impart spirituality to a disciple without

**Inviting grace of
Master**

there being any apparent effort
or sacrifice on the part of the
disciple, but these are always
cases in which the disciple has earned the right to this
favour by his associations and endeavours in past lives.
The love and devotion which the disciple may have
felt for the Master through his past lives has formed
a *deep connection between him and the Master,* so that
the *awakening of spiritual longing in the disciple has its
counterpart in the grace and help which flow to him from
the Master*. It is through his own past unbinding *Karma*
that a person invites the grace of the Master, just as it
is through his own binding *Karma* that he invites upon
himself the pleasure and pain as well as the good and
evil of which he is the recipient in this life.

As a rule, the person who has entered the Path
gradually advances until he attains the goal, but this

**Spiritual progress
requires active effort**

does not apply to those who
have not definitely entered
the Path or have no Master to

guide them. Through their chaotic pursuits of several lifetimes most persons are likely to go further away from the goal by the heaping up of binding *sanskaras,* hence spiritual progress cannot be said to be *automatic* in the sense that it will come about without the active efforts of the person concerned.

Sooner or later the logic of experience gathered through several lives drives everyone to enter the Path and seek the highest goal. Once the aspirant enters the

Danger of falling back

Path he usually goes forward with steady progress. As he advances on the Path he often develops certain latent capacities which enable him not only to experience consciously the inner subtle and mental worlds, but also to manipulate the forces and powers available on the higher planes. But *the crossing of the first few planes does not necessarily ensure safe and steady progress.* There are many pit-falls on the Path itself, and unless there is the assured guidance of a Master, the aspirant is in danger of falling back.

From the first few planes the aspirant may have such a set-back. Instead of going ahead towards God he may suffer severe retrogression. In an exceptional

Yoga-bhrasta

case the aspirant of the fourth plane may, through erroneous *Karma,* invite upon himself such a fall that it takes ages for him to return to his earlier point of progress. The aspirant who has such a fall is known as a *yoga-bhrasta. Even the yogis are subject to the unyielding law of Karma which knows no exceptions, concessions or preferences.* It is only when the aspirant has the advantage of guidance by a Perfect Master that the spiritual journey is rendered safe and steady, and it is only then that there is no possibility of a fall or retrogression. The Master steers him from negative *Karma* in which he might otherwise become involved.

Treading the spiritual Path continues for several incarnations before the aspirant attains the goal. *Centuries of continued sacrifices, service, self-purification, suffering and determined search have to roll on, if the aspirant is to be spiritually prepared for the final realisation of God.* God-realisation, which is the goal of the reincarnating individual, is never an attainment of a single life. It is always the culmination of his continued endeavour through many lives. Unintelligent *Karma* of many lives has created the bindings of the individual soul, and it has to be undone by the persistent creation of intelligent and unbinding *Karma* carried on for many lives.

The power that keeps the individual soul bound to the wheel of life and death is its thirst for separate existence, which is a condition for a host of cravings connected with objects and experiences of the world of duality. *It is for the fulfillment of cravings that the ego-mind keeps on incarnating itself.*

Power behind reincarnations is craving

When all forms of craving disappear, the impressions which create and enliven the ego-mind disappear. With the disappearance of these impressions, the ego-mind itself is shed with the result that there is only the realisation of the one eternal, unchanging Oversoul or God, Who is the only reality. *God-realisation is the end of the incarnations of the ego-mind because it is the end of its very existence.* As long as the ego-mind exists in some form, there is an inevitable and irresistible urge for incarnations. *When there is cessation of the ego-mind, there is cessation of incarnations in the final fulfillment of Self-realisation.*

The life of the reincarnating individual has many events and phases. The wheel of life makes its ceaseless rounds, lifting the individual to the heights or bring-

Destiny of reincarnations

ing him down from high positions. It thus contributes to the enrichment of his experience. Ideals left unattained in one life are pursued further in the next life; things left undone are finished; the edges left by incomplete endeavour are rounded up; wrongs are eventually set right. The accounts of give and take between persons receive renewed adjustment by the repayment of *Karmic* debts and the recovery of *Karmic* dues. At last, *out of the ripeness of experience and through the dissolution of the ego-mind, the soul enters into the sole unity of Divine Life. In this Divine Life there is neither the binding of giving nor the binding of taking, because the soul has completely transcended the consciousness of separateness or duality.*

The drama of the continued life of the individual soul has many acts. From the viewpoint of the worldly existence of the soul, a curtain may be said to be drawn

Analogy of drama

over its life after the closing of each act. But no act yields its real significance if it is regarded as complete in itself. It has to be viewed from its wider context as being a link between the acts already performed and the acts still to come. Its meaning is entwined with the theme of the whole drama of which it is a part. The end of the act is not the end of the progressive theme. *The actors disappear from the stage of earth only to reappear again in new capacities and new contexts.*

The actors are so engrossed in their respective roles that they treat them as being the be-all and end-

Game of hide and seek

all of all existence. For the major part of their continued life (running into innumerable incarnations), they are unconscious of the closely guarded truth that *the Author of the drama, in His imaginative production, Himself became all the actors and played the game of hide and seek in order to come into full and conscious possession of His own creative infinity.* Infinity has to go through the illusion of finitehood to know Itself as Infinity, and the Author has to go through the phases of the actors to know Himself as the Author of *the greatest detective story, worked out through the cycles of creation.*

We Must Live for God and Die for God

THIS war* is a necessary evil; it is in God's plan, which is to awaken humanity to higher values. If humanity fails to profit by the lessons of the war, it will have suffered in vain. This war is teaching that even the man in the street can rise to the greatest heights of sacrifice for the sake of a selfless cause. It is also teaching that all the mundane things of the world—wealth, possessions, power, fame, family and even the very tenor of life on earth—are transitory and devoid of lasting value. *Through the lessons which they bring, the incidents of war shall win man over for God, Who is the Truth,* and they will initiate him into a new life which is inspired by true and lasting values. People are making unlimited sacrifices and enduring untold sufferings for the sake of their country or political ideology. They are therefore capable of the same sacrifices and endurance for the sake of God or the Truth. All religions have unequivocally claimed man for the life in the Truth; it is sheer folly to fight in the name of religions. It is time that men had a fresh vision of the truth that all life is one and that *God is the only thing which is real and that matters.* God is worth living for and He is also worth dying for. All else is a vain and empty pursuit of illusory values.

---

* World War II

Work for the Spiritual Freedom of Humanity

ALL over the world the spirit of man is crying for freedom. Love of freedom and the search for freedom are the principal characteristics of humanity. *In*

Cry for freedom

all races and in all climes, in all countries and at all times, the watchword for the groping and struggling humanity has always been freedom! There are very few persons however who really understand the full implications of true and unqualified freedom; and there are many who, in their partial understanding of the real conditions of freedom, strive only for the attainment of that kind of existence which gives them a sense of *relative* freedom. Thus, *different persons long for different kinds of freedom according to the different things which they have come to value.*

Freedom to live as one wishes is sought in all departments of life. *This imperative demand for freedom usually expresses itself by fastening upon some external*

Kinds of freedom

conditions of the kind of existence which people wish to lead. Thus those who identify their being with their country seek national or political freedom. Those who are animated by economic purposes seek economic freedom. Those who are inspired by religious aspirations seek freedom of religion. Those who are enthusiastic about sociological or cultural ideology seek freedom of movement and freedom to express the ideals which they cherish and which they wish to propagate. But there are few who realise that the *basic* freedom which alone gives the stamp of true value to any of these different kinds of relative freedom is spiritual freedom. *Even when all the external conditions of a free life are completely fulfilled and guaranteed, the soul of man would still remain in woeful bondage if it had failed to realise spiritual freedom.*

All the different types of freedom which fasten upon some external conditions must, in their very nature, exist within certain limits, for the freedom which

Limits of freedom

an individual or community or state seeks must be consistent with *similar* freedom for *other* individuals, communities or states. *National, economic, religious or cultural freedom expresses itself in and by means of the duality of existence. It lives on duality and is sustained by duality; therefore it has to be relative and limited and cannot be infinite.* It exists in varying *degrees,* and even when it is won through persistent effort, it cannot be a permanent attainment since the external conditions which have once been secured are not secured forever, but are capable of deteriorating in the course of time.

Only spiritual freedom is absolute and unlimited. When it is won through persistent effort, it is secured forever. Though spiritual freedom can and does express

Spiritual freedom alone can be unlimited

itself in and through the duality of existence, it is grounded in the realisation of the inviolable unity of all life, and is sustained by it. One important condition of spiritual freedom is freedom from all wanting. It is want that fetters life through attachment to conditions which would fulfill that want; if there is no want, there is no dependence or limitation. The soul is enslaved through wanting. *When the soul breaks asunder the shackles of wanting, it emancipates itself from its bondage to the bodies, mind and ego.* This is the spiritual freedom which brings with it the final realisation of the unity of all life and puts an end to all doubts and worries.

It is only in spiritual freedom that one can have *abiding happiness and unimpaired self-knowledge.* It is only in spiritual freedom that there arises the supreme certainty of Truth. It is only in **Importance of spiritual freedom** spiritual freedom that there is the final ending of sorrow and limitation. It is only in spiritual freedom that one can live for all, and yet be detached in the midst of all activities. Any lesser type of freedom is comparable to a house which is built on sand, and any lesser type of attainment is frought with the fear of decay. Therefore there is no gift greater than the gift of spiritual freedom, and there is no task more important than the task of helping others to achieve spiritual freedom. Those who have understood the supreme importance of spiritual freedom have not only to strive for it for themselves, but also to share the God-given duty of helping others to win it.

Those who are inspired by a spirit of selfless service are quick to render unto humanity all possible help through provision of the necessities of life like clothes **True service** and shelter, food and medicine, education and other amenities of civilization. In pursuing the path of duty they are not only prepared to fight for the weak against aggression and oppression, but also to lay down their very lives for the sake of others. All these types of service are great and good, but from the ultimate point of view, the help which secures spiritual freedom for humanity surpasses them all; it is insuperable in importance.

The way to help others attain spiritual freedom is far different from the way of rendering other types of help. For the hungry you can provide food, and they

Way to help others attain spiritual freedom

have only to eat it. For the naked you can provide clothes, and they have only to wear them. For the homeless ones you can provide houses, and they have only to dwell in them. For those who are in the agonies of spiritual bondage, however, there is no *ready-made provision* which can give them immediate relief. *Spiritual freedom has to be won by oneself for oneself through watchful and unfailing war against the lower self and the lower desires.* Those who would be soldiers in the cause of Truth have to help all, not only in launching upon the thrilling enterprise of attaining victory over oneself, but also in every step which they take towards that attainment. There is no other way of sharing their burden.

I have full confidence that you, my devotees, will share this burden. Many of you, for years together, have obeyed my orders and carried out my instructions,

The call

through faith in me and love for me. You have stuck to me and my spiritual cause through storm and stress and thick and thin. Now the time has come for you to offer all your services in my mission of helping humanity to tread the spiritual path to realise God. The eternal truth that God alone is real has to be clearly understood and unreservedly accepted, and it has to be unequivocally expressed through words and deeds. *In the full realisa-*

tion of the Truth, man shall attain spiritual freedom. No *sacrifice is too big to set man free from spiritual bondage and help him to inherit the Truth which alone shall bring abiding peace to all, and which alone will sustain an un-assailable sense of universal fellowhood, cemented by the ungrudging love of all, for all, as expressions of the same reality.* In this God-willed divinely-planned and predes-tined task of bringing spiritual freedom to humanity, you, my devotees, have to help me, even at the cost of life. In your duty of helping others to find God, you have to welcome every type of suffering and sacrifice.

The Task for Spiritual Workers

I am very happy that, in response to my call, you have gathered to receive my message to you. On the Path, the most important condition of discipleship is readiness to work for the spiritual cause of bringing humanity closer and closer to the realisation of God. I am glad to note that through faith and love for me you have whole-heartedly offered yourselves to share in my universal work of *spiritualising the world.* I have full confidence that *you will not only inherit for yourselves the Truth which I bring, but also become enthusiastic and valiant torch-bearers for humanity, which is enveloped in deep ignorance.*

Be the torch-bearers for humanity

Because of its supreme importance for the true and final well-being of humanity, spiritual work has a natural and imperative claim on all who love humanity. It is therefore very necessary to be quite clear about its nature. The whole world is firmly established in *the false idea of separateness,* and being caught up in the illusion of duality, it is subject to all the complexities of duality. *The spiritual workers have to redeem the world from the throes of imagined duality by bringing home to it the truth of the unity of all life.*

Nature of spiritual work

The root-cause of the illusion of manyness is that

the soul, in its ignorance, identifies itself with its bodies or with the ego-mind. The gross and subtle bodies

Origin of manyness

as well as the ego-mind of the mental body are all *mediums* for experiencing the different states of the world of duality, but they cannot be the mediums for knowing the true nature of the soul, which is above them all. By being identified with the bodies or the ego-mind, the soul gets caught up in the ignorance of manyness. *The soul in all the bodies and ego-mind is really one undivided existence, but as it gets mixed up with these bodies and ego-mind which are only its vehicles, it considers itself as limited and looks upon itself as being only one among the many of creation instead of looking upon itself as being the only one reality without a second.*

Every soul is eternally and inviolably one with the one undivided and indivisible universal Soul which is the sole reality. Yet *false identification with the bodies*

States of conscious-ness

or the ego-mind creates the illusion of manyness and of differentiation within the whole. The bodies or the ego-minds are only the mediums or the vehicles of consciousness, and *as the soul experiences the different planes of creation through its different mediums or vehicles, it goes through different states of consciousness.*

Most souls are unconscious of their true nature as God, Who is the unity and reality of all souls. God-realisation is only *latently* present in them, since in

God-realisation

them it has not yet come to be experienced consciously. Those who have cast off the veil of duality *experience the soul through itself independently of any mediums or vehicles.* In this experience *the soul consciously knows itself as being identical with God, Who is the unity and the reality of all souls.* Life in the Truth of the unity of all brings with it freedom from all limitations and sufferings. It is *the self-affirmation of the Infinite as infinite.* In this state of spiritual freedom and perfection, the ego-life is finally and completely surrendered in order to experience and release the Divine Life in the Truth, and God is known and affirmed as *the only reality which is worth living for.*

To realise God is to dwell in eternity; it is a *timeless experience.* But spiritual work must be done for the souls who are caught up in the mazes of creation which is

Importance of time

bound by time. *Spiritual workers cannot afford to ignore the element of time in creation.* To ignore time would be to ignore the spiritual work itself. It is imperative to be discriminatingly aware of the flow of time in creation, and *to appreciate fully the supreme importance of the moment in the near future which shall witness the universal dispensation of the Truth of spiritual wisdom.*

The task for spiritual workers is to help me in this universal dispensation of the Truth to suffering humanity. You have not only to prepare humanity to receive

Warning to spiritual workers

this Truth, but also to get established in it. It is extremely important to remember that *you can help others to gain spiritual freedom and to come out of the illusion of duality, only if you yourself do not miss this idea of unity while working for others who are inclined to create divisions where they do not exist and who allow no respite to spiritual workers.*

The minds of people have to be completely purged of all forms of selfishness and narrowness if they are to inherit the *life in eternity* which I bring. It is by no

Obstacles in spiritual work means an easy task to persuade people to give up their selfishness and narrowness. It is not by accident that people are divided into the rich and the poor, the pampered and the neglected, the rulers and the ruled, the leaders and the masses, the oppressors and the oppressed, the high and the low, the winners of laurels and the recipients of ignominy. These differences have been created and sustained by those who, through their spiritual ignorance, are attached to them and who are so much settled in *perverse thinking and feeling* that they are not even conscious of their perversity. They are accustomed to look upon life as divided into inviolable compartments, and they are unwilling to give up their *separative* attitude. *When you launch upon your spiritual work you will be entering into a field of divisions to which people desperately cling, which they accentuate and which they strive to perpetuate consciously or unconsciously.*

Mere condemnation of these divisions will not enable you to destroy them. *The divisions are being nourished by separative thinking and feeling, which can* **Win them over for Truth** *yield only to the touch of love and understanding. You have to win people to the life of Truth; you cannot coerce them into spirituality.* It is not enough that you should have unimpaired friendliness and untarnished good will in your own hearts. If you are to succeed in your work, you have to bring home to them the faith and the conviction that you are helping them to redeem themselves from bondage and suffering and to realise the highest, to which they are rightful heirs. There is no other way to help them attain spiritual freedom and enlightenment.

HINTS FOR SPIRITUAL WORKERS

For rendering spiritual help you should have a clear understanding of the following four points:

(i) Apparent descent to the lower level:
It may often be necessary for you to *apparently* descend to the lower level of those whom you are trying to help. Though your purpose is to raise people to the higher level of consciousness, they might fail to profit by what you say if you do not talk in terms which they understand. What you convey to them through thought-feeling should not go over their heads. They are bound to miss it unless you adapt it to their capacity and experience. However, it is equally important to remember that while doing this, you should not *actually* lose your own high level of understanding. You will change your approach and technique as they gradually arrive at deeper and deeper understanding, and your apparent descent to the lower level will be only temporary.

(ii) Spiritual understanding ensures all-sided progress:
You must not divide life into departments and then begin to deal with each department separately and exclusively. *Departmental thinking is often an obstacle to integral vision.* Thus, if you divide life into politics, education, morality, material advancement, science, art, religion, mysticism and culture, and then think exclusively of only one of these aspects, the solutions which you bring to life can neither be satisfactory nor final. But if you succeed in awakening spiritual inspiration and understanding, progress in all these departments of

life is bound to follow automatically. As spiritual workers you will have to aim at providing a complete and real solution for all the individual and social problems of life.

(iii) Spiritual progress consists in the spontaneous growth of understanding from within:
As spiritual workers, you have also to remember that the spiritual wisdom which you desire to convey to others is already latently present in them, and that you have only to be instrumental in unveiling that spiritual wisdom. *Spiritual progress is not a process of accumulating from without; it is a process of unfoldment from within. The Master is absolutely necessary for anyone to arrive at self-knowledge, but the true significance of the help given by the Master consists in the fact that he enables others to come into the full possession of their own latent possibilities.*

(iv)   Some questions are more important than answers:
You, as spiritual workers, must not lose sight of the real work which the Masters desire to get done through you. When it is clearly understood that spiritual wisdom is latent in all, you will no longer be anxious to provide others with ready-made answers and solutions. In many cases you will be content *to set up for others a new problem or to clarify for others the nature of the problem which they face.* You may have done your duty if you ask them a question which they would not ask of themselves, when placed in some practical situation. In some cases *you will have done your duty if you succeed in putting them in a searching and questioning attitude,* so that they themselves begin to understand and tackle their prob-

lems along more fruitful and creative lines. To give them a deeper point of view, or suggest to them a fruitful line of thought and action, may itself mean much more than thrusting upon them the results of your judgment. The questions which you may help them to formulate for themselves should neither be merely theoretical nor unnecessarily complicated. If they are simple, straight and fundamental, *these questions will answer themselves,* and people will find their own solutions. You will have rendered indispensable and valuable service to them because, without your tactful intervention, they would not have arrived at the solution of their multifarious problems from the *spiritual* point of view.

It has been seen that spiritual workers must necessarily be confronted with many obstacles, but obstacles are meant to be overcome. Even if some of them seem to be insuperable, you have to do *your* best to help others

Overcoming obstacles

irrespective of results or consequences. *Obstacles and their overcoming, success and failure, are all illusions within the infinite domain of Unity. Your task is already done when it is performed wholeheartedly.* You are steadfast and one-pointed in your desire to help my cause of awakening humanity to the sole reality and the ultimate worthwhileness of God and God alone, and you will get many opportunities for spiritual work. There is ample scope for work in this field.

You must do your work without worrying about consequences irrespective of success or failure, but you may be sure that the result of work done in this spirit

Outcome of spiritual work

and with this understanding is sure. *Through the untiring activities of spiritual workers, humanity shall be initiated into the new life of abiding peace and dynamic harmony, unconquerable faith and unfading bliss, immortal sweetness and incorruptible purity, creative love and infinite understanding.*

Qualifications of the Aspirant

PART I
ENTERING INTO THE REALITIES
OF INNER LIFE

THOUGH God-realisation is the ultimate destiny of all persons, there are very few who have the necessary preparation for the early fulfillment of that glorious destiny. The mind of the **Value and limitations of external conformity** worldly minded is darkened by a thick layer of accumulated *sanskaras* which must be considerably weakened for the aspirant even to enter the Path. The usual method for gradually dissipating the load of *sanskaras* is to follow as strictly as possible the external code of religious rituals and ceremonies. This stage of *external conformity* to religious injunctions or traditions is known as the pursuit of *Shariat* or *Karma-Kanda*. It covers actions like the offering of daily prayers, visiting of holy places, performance of duties prescribed by scriptures and observance of well established rules of the ethical codes generally accepted by the moral consciousness of the times. *The stage of external conformity is useful in its own way as a spiritual discipline; but it is by no means free from evil effects, for it not only tends to make a man dry, rigid and mechanical, but it often nourishes some kind of* *subtle egotism.* However, most persons are attached to the life of external conformity because they find it the easiest way of *placating their uneasy consciences.*

The soul often spends several lives in gathering the lessons of external conformity; but there always comes a time when it tires of external conformity and

Passing on to realities of inner life

becomes more interested in the realities of the inner life. When the worldly man takes to this higher kind of search he might be said to have become an aspirant. Like the insect which passes on through metamorphosis to the next stage of existence, the soul transcends the phase of external conformity *(i.e., Shariat or Karma-Kanda)* and enters upon the path of spiritual emancipation *(i.e., Tarikat or Moksha-Marga).* In this higher phase *the soul is no longer satisfied by external conformity with certain rules, but wants to acquire those qualifications which would make its inner life spiritually beautiful.*

From the point of view of the realities of inner life, the life of external conformity may often be spiritually barren, and a life which deviates from such rigid con-

Limitations of conventions

formity may often be spiritually rich. In seeking conformity with established conventions and formality a man is almost always prone to slip into a life of false or illusory values rather than a life which is based upon true and lasting values. What is conventionally recognised need not always be spiritually sound. On the contrary, *many conventions express and embody illusory values since they have come into existence as a result of the working of average minds which are spiritually ignorant.* Illusory values are mostly conventional because they grow into that matrix of mentality which is most common. This does not mean that conventions necessarily embody nothing but illusory values.

Sometimes people stick to unconventional things for no other reason than that they are out of the ordinary. The unusual nature of their pursuits or interests enables them to feel their separateness and difference from others, and to take delight in it. Unconventional things also often generate interest merely through their novelty in contrast with conventional things. *The illusory values of usual things become insipid through familiarity, and the mind then has a tendency to transfer the illusion of value to those things which are not usual instead of trying to discover true and lasting values.* Transcending the stage of external conformity does not imply a merely mechanical and thoughtless change from conventionality to unconventionality. Such change would be essentially in the nature of *reaction* and could in no way contribute towards a life of freedom and truth. *The freedom from conventionality which appears in the life of the aspirant is not due to any uncritical reaction but is due to the exercise of critical thought. Those who would transcend the stage of external conformity and enter into the high life of inner realities must develop the capacity to distinguish between false and true values irrespective of conventionality or unconventionality.*

Freedom from conventions must be based upon critical thought

The rise from *Shariat* or *Karma-Kanda* to *Tarikat* or *Moksha-Marga* is not to be interpreted therefore as being merely a departure from external conformity. It is *not a change from conventionality to idiosyncrasy,* from the usual to the unusual, but it is a change from a life of thoughtless acceptance of es-

Discrimination between true and false

tablished traditions, to a mode of being which is based upon thoughtful appreciation of the difference between the important and the unimportant. *It is a change from a state of implicit ignorance to a state of critical thoughtfulness.* At the stage of mere external conformity the spiritual ignorance of man is often so complete that he does not even realise that he is ignorant. But when the person is being awakened and enters the Path he begins by realising the need for true light. In the initial stages the effort to attain this light takes the form of *intellectual discrimination between the lasting and the transitory, the true and the false, the real and the unreal, the important and the unimportant.*

For the spiritual aspirant, however, it is not enough to exercise merely intellectual discrimination between the false and the true. *Though intellectual discrimination is undoubtedly the basis for all* **Bankruptcy of barren** *further preparation, it yields its* **beliefs** *fruit only when newly perceived values are brought into relation with practical life.* From the spiritual viewpoint, what matters is not *theory* but *practice.* The ideas, beliefs, opinions, views or doctrines which a person might hold intellectually constitute a superficial layer of human personality. Very often a person believes in one thing and does exactly the opposite. *The bankruptcy of barren beliefs is all the more pitiable because the person who feeds upon them often suffers from the delusion that he is spiritually advanced when, in truth, he has not even begun spiritual life.*

Sometimes even a wrong view, which is held with fervour, may indirectly invite an experience that opens out the gates to the spiritual life. Even at the stage of **Dogmas and creeds** *Shariat* or *Karma-Kanda* allegiance to religions is not infrequently a source of inspiration for many selfless and noble acts for, while these dogmas or creeds are blindly accepted, they are often held with a fervour and enthusiasm which supply a dynamic element to the ideology which has been accepted by the person for the moment. Dogmas and creeds, as compared with barren views and doctrines, have the distinct advantage of being embraced not only by the intellect but also by the heart. They cover and affect a wider part of personality than purely theoretical opinions.

Dogmas and creeds generally, however, are as much a source of evil as of good, because in them the guiding vision is clouded owing to degeneration or suspension of critical thinking. If allegiance to creeds and dogmas has sometimes done good to the individual or to the community to which he belongs, it has more often done harm. Though the mind and heart are involved in allegiance to dogmas and creeds, *both* function in such case under the serious handicap of suspension of thought. Hence dogmas and creeds do not contribute to unmixed good.

Cause of evil results of dogmas and creeds

When a person gives up uncritically accepted dogmas and creeds in favour of views and doctrines to which he has devoted thought, there is a certain amount of advance insofar as his mind has now begun to think and critically examine its beliefs. Very often, however, the newly held beliefs are seen to lack the fervour and enthusiasm which characterised allegiance to dogmas and creeds. If these newly held beliefs lack motive power, they belong only to the superficial aspect of life and they hang loosely upon the person like an overcoat. The mind has been emancipated from

Need for putting theory into practice

the domination of uncultured emotion, but this is often achieved by sacrificing the co-operation of the heart. *If the results of critical thought are to be spiritually fruitful, they must again invade and recapture the heart so as to enlist its co-operative functioning.*

In other words, the ideas which have been accepted after critical examination must again be released into active life if they are to yield their full benefit. In the process of practical life they often undergo a healthy transformation and become more soundly interwoven with the very fabric of life.

The transition from external conformity (i.e., Shariat or Karma-Kanda) to the life of inner realities (i.e., Tarikat or Moksha-Marga) involves two steps: (i) freeing the mind

Critical and creative thinking promotes balance of mind and heart

from the inertia of uncritical acceptance based upon blind imitation and stirring it to critical thinking, and (ii) bringing the results of critical and discriminative thinking into practical life. In order to be spiritually fruitful, thinking must be not only critical but creative. Critical and creative thinking leads to spiritual preparation by cultivating those qualities which contribute towards *the perfection and balancing of the mind and the heart and the release of unfettered divine life.*

Qualifications of the Aspirant

PART II
SOME DIVINE QUALITIES

IF the inner life of man is to be harmonious and enlightened he has to develop and express many divine qualities while he is engaged in his daily duties. Each

Qualities necessary for spiritual life interdependent

quality, by itself, may not seem to be extremely important, but it is not correct to consider it apart from its necessary relation with other important qualities. In spiritual life all these qualities implement and support each other; and their inter-connection is so vital that not one of them can be completely ignored without detriment to many other essential qualities. So, considered in its true function, *each of these divine qualities turns out to be absolutely indispensable for a complete life.*

Every man is a rightful heir to the Truth, but he who would inherit it must be spiritually prepared for it, and this spiritual preparation sometimes takes several lives

Patience and persistence

of patient and persistent effort. Therefore, one of the first requirements of the aspirant is that he should combine *unfailing enthusiasm with unyielding patience.* Once a man is determined to realise

the Truth he finds that his path is beset with many difficulties, and there are very few who persist with steady
courage till the very end. It is easy to give up effort when
one is confronted with obstacles. This might be illustrated by a story of a man from Poona. He once read a
spiritual book which impressed him so deeply that he
felt like renouncing everything. He left Poona, went to
a jungle near the city, and sitting under a tree with a ro-
sary in his hand, he began to repeat God's name. He kept
doing this all day in spite of much inconvenience and
dwindling enthusiasm. After sunset he heard from all
sides the cries of animals, and though these cries grew
louder and louder in the gathering darkness of the night
he persisted in his determination. When, however, he
saw through the darkness a huge bear coming towards
him, he fled to save his life and ran for seven miles at
top speed until he fell unconscious in a shop in Poona.
As he regained consciousness he related his adventure
to those who had gathered around him, much to their
amusement; and that finished his mood for renunciation.

Spiritual effort demands not only physical endurance and courage, but also unshrinking forbearance
and unassailable moral courage. The world is caught

**Accepting the world
as it is**

up in *Maya* and is addicted to
false values, therefore *the ways
of the world run counter to the
standards which the aspirant has set for himself.* If he
runs away from the world, that does not help him. He
will again have to come back to the world to develop
that quality which would enable him to face and accept
the world as it is. Very often his Path lies through the
world which he has to serve in spite of not liking its
ways. *If the aspirant is to love and serve the world which*

*does not understand him or even is intolerant towards
him, he must develop infinite forbearance.*

As the aspirant advances on the Path he acquires,
through his contact with the Master, an increasingly
deeper understanding of true love. This makes him

Forbearance

painfully sensitive to those impacts from outside which not
only do not taste of love, but actually bring him into
contact with cold contempt, cynical callousness, agonising apathy and unabating hatred. All these impacts try
his forbearance to the utmost. Even the worldly man
suffers in the world which he occasionally finds indifferent or hostile, but he is thick-skinned and his suffering
is less acute. He does not expect anything much better
from human nature and thinks that these things are
inevitable and incurable. *The aspirant, who has tasted
of a deeper love, knows the hidden possibilities in every
soul, and his suffering is acute because he feels the gulf
between that which is and that which might have been if
only the world had even faintly appreciated the love which
he has begun to understand and cherish.*

The task of forbearance would be easy if the aspirant could become reconciled to the ways of the world
and accept them without challenge. *Having seen the*

**Moral courage and
confidence**

*higher, however, it becomes his
imperative duty to stand by it,
even if the whole world opposes*
him. Loyalty to the higher truth of his own perception
demands unshakable moral courage and readiness to
face the criticism, scorn and even hatred of those who
have not yet begun to open out to the truth. Although
in this uneven struggle he does get unfailing help from
the Master and other co-aspirants, he has to develop
the capacity to fight for the truth *single-handed,* without

relying upon external help all the time. *This supreme moral courage can only come with supreme confidence in oneself and the Master. To love the world and serve it in the ways of the Masters is no game for the weak and faint-hearted.*

Moral courage and self-confidence should be accompanied by *freedom from worry.* There are very few things in the mind which eat up as much energy as worry. It is one of the most dif-

Freedom from worry

ficult things not to worry about anything. Worry is experienced when things go wrong, but in relation to past happenings it is idle merely to wish that they might have been otherwise. *The frozen past is what it is, and no amount of worrying is going to make it other than what it has been.* But the limited ego-mind identifies itself with its *past,* gets entangled with it and keeps alive the pangs of frustrated desires. Thus worry continues to grow into the mental life of man until the ego-mind is burdened by the past. Worry is also experienced in relation to the *future* when this future is expected to be disagreeable in some way. In this case it seeks to justify itself as a necessary part of the attempt to prepare for coping with the anticipated situations. But, *things can never be helped merely by worrying.* Besides, many of the things which are anticipated never turn up, or if they do occur, they turn out to be much more acceptable than they were expected to be. *Worry is the product of feverish imagination working under the stimulus of desires.* It is a living through of sufferings which are mostly our own creation. *Worry has never done anyone any good, and it is very much worse than mere dissipation of psychic energy, for it substantially curtails the joy and fullness of life.*

Among the many things which the aspirant needs

to cultivate there are few which are as important as *cheerfulness, enthusiasm and equipoise,* and these are

Cheerfulness, enthusiasm and equipoise

rendered impossible unless he succeeds in cutting out worry from his life. *When the mind is gloomy, depressed or disturbed its action is chaotic and binding.* Hence arises the supreme need to maintain cheerfulness, enthusiasm and equipoise under all circumstances. All these are rendered impossible unless the aspirant succeeds in cutting out worry from his life. Worry is a necessary resultant of attachment to the past or to the anticipated future, and it always persists in some form or other until the mind is completely detached from everything.

The difficulties in the Path can be overcome only if the aspirant has one-pointedness. If his psychic energies are dissipated in worldly pursuits, the progress he makes

Control and dispassion, conditions for one-pointedness

is very slow. One-pointedness implies dispassion concerning all the allurements of the phenomenal world. The mind must turn away from all temptations and complete control be established over the senses. Hence *control and dispassion are both necessary to attain one-pointedness in the search for true understanding.*

The supreme condition for sure and steady progress on the Path is the benefit of *guidance from the Master.* The Master gives just that guidance and help which is

Availing of the help from the Master

necessary according to the immediate needs of the aspirant. All the Master expects is that the aspirant will try his best for spiritual advancement. He does not expect immediate transformation of consciousness except where the ground is previously ready.

Time is an important factor in spiritual advancement
as it is in all material endeavours. When the Master has
given a spiritual push to the aspirant, he waits till the
help thus given is completely assimilated by him. *An
overdose of spirituality always has an unhealthy reaction,
particularly when it is inopportune. The Master therefore
carefully selects the moment when his intervention is
assured of maximum results; and having intervened, he
waits with infinite patience till the aspirant really needs
further help.*

Qualifications of the Aspirant

THE aspirant always has to be in readiness to serve the cause of humanity. He need not apply himself to any type of work irrespective of his capacity. He has to select that portion of work

Readiness to serve according to aptitude and ability

which he is qualified to do by virtue of his *individual aptitude and abilities*. But whatever service he can render by virtue of his capacity, he renders even when the circumstances are most trying.

The ordeals through which he may have to pass are many, but his determination to serve whenever possible must remain unshaken. *He is not in any way attached to the idea of service, however,*

No claims of limited I"

in the sense of maximum results being secured through himself alone. If any service needs to be rendered he is willing to render it with any amount of sacrifice, but he is never bound by the false idea, "I alone should have the credit for doing it." If the privilege of rendering the service falls to the lot of someone else, he is not envious. If he were to seek opportunities for himself to render service it would be a form of selfishness. In service which really counts in the spiritual life there can be no thought of the self at all. There should be no necessity felt to have something for oneself or of being the one who can give something to others. *The self in all its forms has to be left entirely out of the picture. Service should spring out of the spontaneity of freedom if and when it is necessary; and it has to come in the co-operative spirit in which there is no insistence upon the claims of the limited "I."*

If the aspirant is completely detached from all works and their results he becomes free from the vitiating opposites of the great things and small things.

Freedom from opposites of great and small things

The worldly-minded feel their separative existence through achievements. Therefore they have a natural tendency to judge their achievements in terms of tangible quantities. They grasp at great things and avoid the little things. *From the spiritual point of view, the so-called little things are often seen to be as important as the so-called great things.* The aspirant has no motive to eschew the one and seek the other; therefore he attends to little things with as much zest as to great things.

In the spiritual life even little things matter as much as great things, but the conventions of the world usually fail to recognise this simple truth. By following

Conventions restrict scope of service

conventionally accepted ideas *the scope of possible service to fellow beings gets artificially restricted to those things which are conventionally regarded as important.* So many things which really are of vital importance to life are neglected, with the result that life is spiritually impoverished.

So, in a society which is dominated by merely material conceptions of life, service is interpreted in terms of providing for bread or clothes or other physical amenities of existence. In a society which is responsive to the value of intellectual culture, service is interpreted in terms of spreading learning in different forms. In a society which has developed taste for beauty, service is interpreted in terms of organising the production and distribution of works of art. In a society which is responsive to the ineffable values of the heart, service is interpreted in terms of constructing those channels which will facilitate the culture and expression of the heart. In a society which is alive to the supreme importance of the spirit, service is interpreted in terms of imparting spiritual understanding. Of these different types of service, the service which is concerned with spiritual understanding is the highest, because *spiritual understanding includes the right perspective to all human problems and promotes their solution.*

Accepted values determine fields of service

If there is no spiritual understanding, the desire for rendering service to others is harnessed by limited conceptions. *Service is of two kinds: it consists in adding to the lives of others those things which are really worthwhile, or it consists in removing from the lives of others those handicaps which prevent them from having things which are worthwhile. If our ideas of things which are worthwhile are narrow, the scope of possible service also becomes correspondingly narrow.*

Two kinds of service

The scope of service is not limited to great gestures like giving big donations to public institutions. *They also serve who express their love in little things.* A word that gives courage to a drooping heart or

Little things that matter

a smile that brings hope and cheer in gloom, has as much claim to be regarded as service as onerous sacrifices and heroic self-denials. A glance which wipes out bitterness from the heart and sets it throbbing with a new love is also service, although there may be no thought of service in it. When taken by themselves all these things seem to be small, but life is made up of many such small things. *If these small things were ignored life would be not only unbeautiful but unspiritual.*

Just as the worldly-minded have a tendency to judge positive contributions in terms of magnitudes, so they also make a similar mistake in judging obstacles, handicaps and adversities.

Element of error in worldly estimates

Thus, for most persons, the adversity of another must assume colossal proportions if it is to deserve notice. It is characteristic of the worldly-minded to *give more importance to things that take shape in external and tangible ways than to things which are silent elements of inner life.* Devastating war, for example, is considered to be a greater calamity than lingering lives filled with bitter hatred, though from the purely spiritual point of view, lives filled with bitter hatred are not in any way less evil than devastating war. War assumes so much importance because of the many visual instances of cruelty, but hatred is equally unbeautiful even when it does not materialise itself into outward action. In the same way, epidemics, injuries and the sufferings of the deathbed invite more attention from the worldly-minded than the agonies of the heart which is heavy with the burden of unquenchable desire.

For the aspirant who is eager to serve without any desire for recognition and credit, *everything that thwarts or perverts the release of full life is worthy of attention,*

Field of service is life as a whole

irrespective of whether it is great or small in the opinion of the world. Just as the building up or the collapse of empires has a place in the flow of universal life, so the fleeting moments of sadness also have their own place in it. The importance of the one should not be measured in terms of the other, and the claims of the one should not be ignored for the claims of the other. *The aspirant looks at life as an integral whole, without allowing any part to monopolise his attention at the cost of others.*

Even when the aspirant is rendering a service which is selfless, he keeps constant guard upon his mind. The aspirant must be humble, honest and sincere. The

Service springing from love ensures harmony

service he renders must not be for the sake of mere show, and it should be an outcome of true love. *If the aspirant is inspired by love, his love will enable him to be in complete harmony with other co-workers without being jealous.* If there is not complete harmony amongst the co-workers, the service which is rendered falls short of the spiritual ideal. Further, if the aspirant renders the outward service without a spirit of love, he is acting from a sense of duty, as in many worldly institutions where there are paid workers. In the institutions of the world people work for pay. At best it is a cold sense of duty which prompts them to be efficient. Their work cannot have the inward beauty of work which is spontaneously done out of love.

The aspirant can best assimilate the lessons of true service if he has the good fortune to be in contact with a Master. The Master teaches not through preaching but through example. When the Master is seen in his

Importance of contact with Master capacity of rendering service to humanity, the aspirant is quick to catch that spirit because of his love for the Master. Contact with the Master is also helpful in imbibing the spirit of co-operation which the aspirants can cultivate easily because of their common love for the Master. They serve because the Master wants it. They do the Master's work, not their own, and they do it not of their own accord but because they have been entrusted with that work by the Master. Therefore *they are all free from any ideas of individualistic claims, rights or privileges, being keen only about the Master's work, ready to serve his cause to the best of their ability when they are called upon to do so, and equally ready to hand over that work to another co-aspirant if he can do it better.*

In co-operation of this type the aspirants are in a way serving each other because the Master's work is accepted by them all as their own, and in being useful **Service without fuss** to a co-aspirant in doing the Master's work the aspirant is rendering a service to him as much as to the Master. In such service there can be no bossing because the aspirant is always conscious that it is the Master's work which he has accepted as his own that he is doing. He further knows that, as aspirants, they are all equal, and it is easy for him to cultivate the habit of serving in the spirit of utter humility. If service makes him proud he might as well not have served. *One of the most difficult things to learn is to render service without bossing, without making a fuss about it and without any consciousness of high and low. In the world of spirituality, humility counts at least as much as utility.*

When the Master serves others he does so not because he is attached to the work, but in order to help, and also to set to his disciples an example in selfless

Ideal of service

service. While serving others, he sees himself in them and experiences having served himself. *In his unwaning blissful feeling of oneness the Master knows himself to be at once the Lord of all and the servant of all. He therefore exemplifies the ideal of service in which there is no enslavement, either of him who receives service or of him who renders it.* The aspirant can speedily realise the ideal of true service if he has before him the example of the Master; but *the spiritual preparation of the aspirant can never be termed complete unless he has learned the art of rendering service which gives not boredom but joy, which brings not enslavement but freedom, which does not set claims and counter-claims but springs from the spontaneity of free give and take, which is free from the burden of personal want, and which is sustained by the sense of ever-renewed fulfillment.*

Qualifications of the Aspirant

PART IV
FAITH

ONE of the most important qualifications for the aspirant is faith. There are *three* kinds of faith: (i) *faith in oneself*, (ii) *faith in the Master and* (iii) *faith in* **Faith and its forms** *life*. Faith is so indispensable to life that unless it is present in some degree, life itself would be impossible. *It is because of faith that cooperative and social life becomes possible. It is faith in each other that facilitates a free give and take of love, a free sharing of work and its results.* When life is burdened with unjustified fear of one another it becomes cramped and restricted.

Children have a natural faith in their elders. They instinctively look to them for protection and help without requiring any letters of introduction. This quality **Faith and its counterpart** of trusting others persists in later life unless a person is rudely shocked by others who, through self-interest, deceive and exploit them. So, though faith is natural to man, it grows and flourishes in a society where people are reliable, honest and worthy of faith, and it fades in a hostile environment. Faith in one another becomes complete and steady when it finds its counterpart in those qualities which invite and confirm faith. *Being worthy of the faith which others place in us and having faith in others are two complementary virtues. They are the condition for an unhampered flow and development of individual and collective life.*

Unqualified and implicit faith in each other belongs to the world of ideals. In actual practice it exists only in special cases. Though it is very much to be desired, it

Importance of faith in oneself

cannot come unless the world is populated by persons who deserve unlimited faith. This condition requires a perfect development of the qualities of being reliable, steadfast and invariably helpful. But these qualities which foster mutual faith remain undeveloped unless one has supreme faith in oneself. *If a man has no faith in himself, he cannot develop those qualities which invite and foster faith from others.* The confidence that you can remain loyal under all sorts of trying circumstances to your own perception of the best, is the very foundation of the superstructure of a reliable character.

Unshakable faith in oneself is as rare as implicit faith in some other person. Few have developed it to the degree which ensures effective and constructive con-

Secure basis of self-confidence

trol of oneself. In most persons faith in oneself is always being challenged and undone by the constant experience of one's own frailties and failings which often prove to be unyielding, even when one knows what is right. *The self-confidence which is thus in perpetual danger of being shattered, can be securely established only when the man has before him the vision of the living example of perfection, and has faith in it.*

Faith in the Master becomes all-important because

it nourishes and sustains faith in oneself and faith in life in the very teeth of set-backs and failures, handicaps

Faith in the Master

and difficulties, limitations and failings. Life, as man knows it in himself, or in most of his fellow-men, may be narrow, twisted and perverse, but life as he sees it in the Master is unlimited, pure and untainted. *In the Master, man sees his own ideal realised; the Master is what his own deeper self would rather be. He sees in the Master the reflection of the best in himself which is yet to be, but which he will surely one day attain. Faith in the Master therefore becomes the chief motive-power for realising the divinity which is latent in man.*

True faith is grounded in the deeper experiences of the spirit and the unerring deliverances of purified intuition. It is not to be regarded as the antithesis of criti-

Faith and critical reasoning

cal reason but as the unfailing guide of critical reason. *When critical reason is implemented by a deep and living faith, based on pure intuition, its functioning becomes creative, fruitful and significant instead of barren, ineffective and meaningless.* On the other hand, many forms of naive *credulity* cannot be broken through except by the fearless and free working of critical reason. However, it remains true that critical reason can touch and inform only those forms of faith which are not based upon pure intuition. True faith grounded on pure intuition always remains an imperative which cannot be ultimately reduced to the conclusions of ratiocinative intellect. It is not derived from the limited intellect, but is more fundamental and primary, with the result that it cannot be silenced by any intellectual acrobatics. This does not mean, however, that faith need at any stage be blind, in the sense that it is not allowed to be examined by critical intellect. *True faith is a form of sight and not of blindness. It need not be afraid of the free functioning of critical reason.*

The right of testing the Master through critical reasoning has always been conceded to the disciples; but *if, after testing and being satisfied about the perfec-*

Credulity and doubt

tion of the Master, the disciple shows any wavering of faith, it is a result of a deplorable deficiency in his sincerity of approach and integrity of purpose. As there is much uncritical and undeserved credulity given to claimants of spiritual wisdom, so there is much unjustified wavering of faith in spite of a convincing basis for it in one's own experience. Just as uncritical credulity is ultimately the result of unconscious operation of many worldly wants, so unjustified wavering of faith is also due to the unconscious operation of desires which run contrary to the effective manifestation of a rationalised faith. *In the first case wish is the father of unwarranted belief, and in the second case wish is the father of unwarranted doubt.*

Cravings have a tendency to pervert the functioning of critical reason. *An unwavering faith which is grounded in pure intuition can come only to a mind*

Wavering of faith often due to unconscious cravings

which is free from the pressure of diverse wants. True faith is, therefore, a matter of gradual growth. It grows in proportion to the success which the disciple attains in freeing his consciousness from diverse cravings.

Faith must be carefully distinguished from mere intellectual belief or "opinion." When a person has a good opinion about someone he is said to have a cer-

Beliefs and opinions

tain kind of faith in him. But this kind of opinion does not have that spiritual potency which belongs to a living faith in the Master. The beliefs and opinions of a person often constitute a very superficial layer of the human psyche. They do not have any integral relationship with the deeper psychic forces. *They remain in one region of the mind without bringing about any radical changes in the core of personality, which determines the attitude to life.* People hold such beliefs just as they wear clothes. In times of emergency they tend to change their clothes to suit their immediate purposes. In such cases, *beliefs are unconsciously determined by other purposes; the purposes are not consciously determined by beliefs.*

Living faith, on the other hand, has the most vital and integral relation with all the deeper forces and purposes of the psyche. It is not "held" superficially, nor does it hang, like mere intellec-
Living faith creatively dynamic tual beliefs, in the periphery of consciousness. On the contrary, living faith becomes a powerful factor that reconstructs the entire psyche; it is *creatively dynamic. There is no thought unenlivened by it, no feeling unillumined by it, no purpose which is not recast by it.* Such living faith in the Master becomes, for the disciple, a supreme source of inspiration and unassailable self-confidence. It expresses itself primarily through the spirit of active reliance upon the Master and not merely through some opinion about him. *Living faith is not a sort of certificate given by the disciple to the Master; it is an active attitude of confidence in the Master, expressing itself not only through implicit and trustful expectation of help from the Master, but also through the spirit of self-surrender and dedication.*

Such fruitful and living faith in the Master is always born of some deep *experience* which the Master imparts to the deserving disciple. It is fundamentally different

Living faith grounded in experience from the beliefs which people hold either through *uncritical acceptance or superficial thinking.* Mere intellectual beliefs for the most part have very little spiritual importance. The Master, therefore, is utterly unconcerned with whether the disciple believes in him or in someone else: and he is equally unconcerned with whether the disciple, at any moment, does or does not believe in him. If in some fortunate cases the Master, through his benign intervention, wins for himself the living faith of the disciple (as distinguished from mere belief), it is because he knows that the disciple will be helped through it.

Just as the disciple is testing the Master's capacity to guide him, so the Master in turn is testing the disciple's integrity of purpose. The Master is unconcerned whether the disciple doubts him or has faith in him. What he tests is **Testing the disciple** whether the disciple is or is not sincere and whole-hearted in his spiritual search and pursuit. *The Master is not at all interested in giving proof of his own divinity to the disciple, except when he feels that such proof is likely to be unfailingly useful and unavoidably necessary for the spiritual benefit of one who has surrendered himself to him.*

Maya

PART I
FALSE VALUES

EVERYONE wants to know and realise the Truth, but Truth cannot be known and realised as Truth unless ignorance is known and realised as being ignorance. Hence arises the importance of understanding *Maya* or the principle of ignorance. People read and hear much about *Maya*, but few understand what it really is. It is not enough to have a superficial understanding of *Maya;* it is necessary that *Maya* should be understood as it is, *i.e.,* in its reality. *To understand Maya or the principle of ignorance is to know half of the Truth of the universe.* Ignorance in all its forms must disappear if the soul is to be established in the state of self-knowledge. Therefore *it is imperatively necessary for man to know what is false, to know it to be false and to get rid of the false by knowing it to be false.*

Importance of understanding falsehoods of *Maya*

What is the essential nature of a falsehood? If the true is known as being true or if the false is known as being false, there is no falsehood but only a form of knowledge. *Falsehood consists in taking the true as being false*

Essence of falsehood

or the false as being true, i.e., in considering something to be other than what in itself it really is. Falsehood is an error in judging the nature of things.

Broadly speaking there are *two* kinds of knowledge: (i) purely intellectual judgments about the facts of existence, and (ii) judgments of valuation which

Two kinds of knowledge

imply the appreciation of the worth or importance of things. Purely intellectual judgments or beliefs derive their importance from being related to values in some way. Divorced from values, they have very meagre importance in themselves. For example, no one takes much interest in counting exactly the number of leaves on a particular tree, although from the purely theoretical point of view such information would be a form of knowledge. Such information or knowledge is treated as unimportant because it is not vitally connected with other values. Intellectual knowledge becomes important (i) when it enables man to realise certain values by giving him control over the *means* to their realisation, or (ii) when it *enters into valuation itself as an important factor, modifying or in some other way affecting the accepted values*.

Just as there are two kinds of judgment, there are two kinds of falsehood: (i) mistakes in accepting as facts those things which are not facts, and (ii) mis-

Three mistakes in valuation

takes in valuation. Mistakes in valuation can be committed in three ways: (a) in taking as important that which is unimportant, or (b) in taking as unimportant that which is important, or (c) in giving to a thing an importance which is other than the importance which it really has. All these falsehoods are creations of *Maya*.

Although *Maya* includes all falsehoods from the spiritual point of view, there are some falsehoods which count and some falsehoods which do not count

Price of mistakes in valuation

very much. If a person takes a throne to be higher than it is, it would be a falsehood, but one which does not matter very much. On the other hand, if a person regards the throne as the be-all and the end-all of his life, that would be a falsehood which substantially affects the course and significance of his life. *On the whole, mistakes in valuation are far more effective in misguiding, perverting and limiting life than mistakes in purely intellectual judgments about certain objective facts.*

Mistakes in valuation arise owing to the influence of subjective desires or wants. *True values* are values which belong to things *in their own right.* They are *in-*

False values due to influence of subjec- tive wants

trinsic, and because they are intrinsic, they are *absolute* and *permanent* and are *not liable to change from time to time or from person to person. False values are derived from desires or wants;* they are *dependent upon subjective factors,* and being dependent upon subjective factors, they are *relative* and *impermanent* and are *liable to change from time to time and from person to person.*

For example, a man who is very thirsty and is in a desert like the Sahara thinks that nothing is more precious than water, while the man who has at hand

Examples

abundance of water and who is not very thirsty, does not attach the same importance to water. In the same way, the man who is hungry considers food very important, but the man who has had a full dinner does not even think of food until he is hungry. The same thing applies to other lusts and longings which *project imaginary and relative values* onto those objects which will fulfill those lusts and longings.

The value of sense-objects is great or small according to the intensity or urgency with which they are desired. If these lusts and longings increase, the corresponding objects assume greater importance. If they subside in their intensity or urgency, the objects also lose much of their importance. If the lusts and longings appear intermittently, those objects retain *possible* value when the lusts and longings are latent, and *actual* value when they are manifested. All these are false values because they are inherent in the objects themselves. When in the light of true knowledge all the lusts and longings disappear completely, objects vested with importance through the working of these lusts and longings immediately lose all their borrowed importance and appear meaningless.

False values derivative and relative

Now *just as a coin which is not in current use is treated as false, though it has a kind of existence, so the objects of lusts and longings when seen in their emptiness are treated as false, though these objects might continue to have some kind of recognition.* They are all there, and they may be known and seen, but they no longer *mean* the same thing. They hold false promise of fulfillment to an imagination which is perverted by lusts and longings, but to the tranquil and steady perception they are seen to have no importance when they are considered separate from the soul.

Emptiness of sense-objects

When a beloved one dies there is sorrow and loneliness, but this sense of loss is rooted in attachment to the form independently of the soul. It is the form which has

Taking as important that which is unimportant

vanished, not the soul. The soul is not dead; in its true nature it has not even passed away, for it is everywhere. But through attachment to the body, the form was considered as important. All longings, desires, emotions and thoughts were centred upon the form; and when, through death, the form disappears, there is a vacuum which expresses itself through missing the departed one. *If the form as such had not come to be surcharged with false importance, there would be no sorrow in missing the one who has passed away.* The feeling of loneliness, the lingering memory of the beloved, the longing that he should still be present, the tears of bereavement and the sighs of separation—they are all due to false valuation, the working of *Maya.* When an unimportant thing is regarded as important, we have one principal manifestation of the working of *Maya*. From the spiritual point of view it is a form of ignorance.

On the other hand, the working of *Maya* also expresses itself by *making an important thing look unimportant.* From the spiritual point of view the only thing

Taking as unimportant that which is important

which has importance is God. Very few persons are really interested in God for His own sake. If the worldly minded turn to God at all, it is mostly for their own selfish and mundane purposes. *They seek the gratification of their own desires, hopes and even revenges through the intervention of the God of their imagination. They do not seek God as Truth.* They long for all things except the only Truth, which they regard as unimportant. This again is the blinding of vision caused by the working of *Maya.*

People pursue their happiness through everything except God, Who is the only unfailing source of abiding joy.

The working of *Maya* also expresses itself by making the mind *give to a thing an importance which is other than the importance which it really has.* This happens

Giving wrong importance

when rituals, ceremonies and other external religious practices are considered to be ends in themselves. They have their own value as means, as vehicles of life, as a medium of expression; but as soon as they assume claims in their own right, they are being given an importance which is other than the one which belongs to them. When they are considered important in themselves, they bind life instead of serving the purpose of expressing it. *When the inessential is allowed to predominate over the essential, we have the third principal form of ignorance concerning valuation.* This again is the working of *Maya.*

Maya

PART II
FALSE BELIEFS

THE shackles which hold the soul in spiritual bond-age consist chiefly of wrong values or falsehoods concerning valuation. Some falsehoods, of the nature

False values and beliefs are clutches of *Maya*

of wrong beliefs, also play an important part in holding the soul in spiritual bondage. False beliefs implement false values,

but they in turn gather strength from false values in which the soul has been hung up. All false beliefs are as much creations of *Maya* as are false values, and *are among the clutches which Maya uses in order to hold the soul in ignorance.*

Maya becomes irresistible by taking possession of the very seat of knowledge, which is human intellect. It is difficult to surmount *Maya* because, with the intel-

Intellect plays into the hands of *Maya*

lect under its sway, *Maya* cre-ates barriers and upholds false beliefs and illusions. It creates

barriers to the realisation of the Truth by persistent attempts to sustain and justify erroneous beliefs. *The intellect which functions in freedom prepares the way to the Truth, but the intellect which plays into the hands of*

Maya creates obstacles to true understanding.

The false beliefs created by *Maya* are so deep-rooted and strong that they seem to be self-evident. They take on the garb of veritable truths and are ac-

False beliefs may seem self-evident

cepted without question. For example, man believes that he is his physical body. Ordinarily it never occurs to him that he may be something other than his body. Identification with the physical body is assumed by him instinctively without requiring proof, and he holds the belief all the more strongly because it is *independent of rational proof.*

Man's life has been centred round the physical body and its desires. To give up the belief that he is the physical body involves the giving up of all the desires

Identification with physical body

pertaining to the physical body and the false values which they imply. The belief that he is his physical body is conducive to the physical desires and attachments; but the belief that he is other than his physical body runs counter to accepted desires and attachments. Therefore the belief that he is his physical body becomes *natural.* It is easy to hold and difficult to uproot. On the other hand, belief that he is something other than his physical body seems to call for convincing proof. It is difficult to hold and easy to resist. All the same, when the mind is unburdened of all physical desires and attachments, the belief that he is his physical body is seen to be false and the belief that he is something other than his body is seen to be true.

Even when a person succeeds in shedding the false belief that he is the physical body, he remains a victim of the false belief that he is his *subtle body.* His life is then centred round the subtle body and *its* desires. To

Identification with subtle body

give up the belief that he is the subtle body involves the giving up of all desires pertaining to the subtle body and the false values which they imply. Therefore the belief that he is his subtle body now becomes natural for him, and the belief that he is something other than his subtle body seems to call for convincing proof. But when the mind is unburdened of all desires and attachments pertaining to the subtle body, the person gives up the false belief that he is his subtle body as readily as he gave up the false belief that he was his physical body.

This is not the end of false beliefs however. Even when a person abandons the false belief that he is his subtle body he cherishes the illusory belief that he is his

Identification with ego-mind

ego-mind or the mental body. *Man cherishes false belief because he relishes it. Throughout his long life as an individual soul he has clung fondly to the false idea of his separate existence. All his thoughts and emotions and activities have repeatedly assumed and confirmed but one affirmation, viz., the existence of the separate "I." To surrender the false belief that he is the ego-mind is to surrender all that has seemed to constitute his very existence.*

In surrendering the false belief that he is his physical or subtle body it is necessary to surrender various desires and attachments. It is a giving up of something

Shedding last falsehood

one has had for a long time. In surrendering the false belief that he is his ego-mind, he is called upon to surrender the very core of what he has thought himself to be. To shed this last vestige of falsehood is, therefore, the most difficult thing. But *this last falsehood is no more lasting than the earlier falsehoods which had seemed to be unchallengeable certainties. It also has its ending, and it is shed when the soul renounces its craving for separate existence.*

When the soul knows itself to be different from the physical and gross bodies as well as the mind, it knows itself to be infinite. *As Soul, it does nothing, it merely IS.*

Soul is beyond thinking and doing

When the mind is added onto the soul, it appears to think. When the subtle body is added onto the soul with the mind, it appears to desire. When the gross body is added onto all these, the soul appears to be engaged in actions. The belief that the soul is doing anything is a false belief. For example, a man believes that *he* is sitting in the chair, but in fact it is the body which is sitting in the chair. The belief that the soul is sitting in the chair is due to identification with the physical body. In the same way a man believes that *he* is thinking, but in fact it is the mind which is thinking. The belief that the soul is thinking is due to identification with the mind. It is the mind which thinks and the body which sits. The soul is neither engaged in thinking nor in any other physical actions.

Of course, it is not mere mind or mere body which does the thinking or other physical actions, for mere mind and mere body do not exist. They exist as illu-

Belief that soul is agent of actions is false

sions of the soul, and it is when the soul falsely identifies itself with them that the thinking or the doing of things occurs. *The soul, mind and body taken together constitute the agent of actions or the limited "I,"* but the soul in its true nature is neither responsible for thinking nor for actions. The illusion that the soul is the mind or the body and the illusion that the soul is the agent of thinking or actions is created by *Maya* or the principle of ignorance.

In the same way, the belief that the soul experiences the pleasures and the pains of life or is going through the opposites of experience is also false. The

Belief that soul is subject of dual experience is false

soul is beyond the opposites of experience, but it does not know itself as such, and so it takes on the experiences which are characteristic of the opposites because of identification with the mind and the body. The soul which is mixed up with the mind and the body becomes the recipient of pains and pleasures. Thus all the pleasures and the pains to which a man is subject are rooted in ignorance. *When a man thinks that he is the most miserable person in the world he is embracing an illusion which comes into existence through ignorance or Maya.* He is really not unhappy but imagines that he is unhappy, because he identifies himself with the mind and the bodies. Of course, it is not the mind by itself or the bodies by themselves which can have any experiences of the opposites. *It is the soul and the mind and the bodies taken together that become the subject of dual experience; but the soul, in its true nature, is beyond the opposites of experience.*

Thus it is the mind and the bodies that constitute the agent of activities and the subject of dual experiences. However, they do not assume this double role in

Nature of ensoulment of mind and bodies

their own right, but only when they are taken along with the soul. *It is the mind and the bodies which are "ensouled" that become the agent of activities or the subject of dual experience. The process of "ensoulment" is based upon ignorance, for the soul in its true nature is eternally unqualified, unmodified and unlimited. It appears to be qualified, modified and limited through ignorance or the working of Maya.*

Maya

COUNTLESS are the falsehoods which a *Maya*-ridden man embraces in the stupor of ignorance, but *from the very beginning, falsehoods carry within them-*

Discerning falsehood

selves their own insufficiency and bankruptcy. Sooner or later they are known to be falsehoods. This brings us to the question, "How do we discern the falsehood as falsehood?" There is no way out of falsehood except by knowing it as falsehood, but this knowledge of falsehood as falsehood would never come unless it were in some way latent in falsehood from the very beginning.

The acceptance of falsehood is always a bedridden compromise. Even in the very depths of ignorance the soul gives some kind of challenge to falsehood. However

In falsehood there is suspicion and fear

feeble and inarticulate it might seem to be in its initial stages, it is the beginning of that search

for the Truth which ultimately annihilates all falsehood and all ignorance. *In the acceptance of a falsehood there is an ever-growing restlessness—a deep suspicion and a vague fear.* For example, when a man considers himself and others to be identical with the gross body, he cannot completely reconcile himself to this belief. In embracing this false belief there is fear of death and fear of losing others. If a man depends for his happiness only upon the possession of forms, he knows in his heart that he is building his castles on shifting sands, that this surely is not the way to abiding happiness, that the support to which he so desperately clings may give way any day. So, he is deeply suspicious of his grounds.

Man is restlessly aware of his own insecurity. He knows that something is wrong somewhere and that he is counting upon *false* hopes. Falsehood is treacherously unreliable. Man simply cannot afford to embrace it forever. He might as well garland himself with a poisonous snake or go to sleep on the top of a volcano which is only temporarily inactive. *A falsehood bears the hall-mark of being incomplete and unsatisfactory, temporary and provisional. It points to something else. It appears to the person to be hiding something which is greater and truer than what it seems to be. Falsehood betrays itself, and in doing so leads man on to know the truth.*

Falsehood betrays itself

Falsehoods are of two types: (1) those which arise due to *irregular and loose* thinking, and (2) those which arise due to *vitiated* thinking. Falsehoods which arise due to irregular thinking are less harmful than falsehoods which arise from vitiated thinking. The untruths of a purely intellectual nature arise because of some *mistake in the application of the intellect,* but falsehoods which count from the spiritual point of view arise because of *the vitiation of the intellect through the operation of blinding and unarguing*

Two types of falsehood

desires.

The difference between these two types of false-hood may be brought out by a *physiological analogy.* Some troubles of the vital organs of the body are *func-*

Analogy of functional and structural troubles

tional and some troubles are *structural.* Functional dis-eases arise because of some irregularity in the functioning of a vital organ. In these cases there is nothing seriously wrong with the struc-ture of the vital organ. It has merely become sluggish or irregular and needs only slight stimulation or correction in order to function properly. In structural diseases the disease comes into existence because of the develop-ment of some deformity in the structure or constitution of the vital organ. In these cases the fault of the vital organ is of a much graver nature. It has become dam-aged or rendered inefficient due to some tangible factor which has entered into the very constitution of the vital organ. Both types of troubles can be corrected, but it is far easier to correct merely functional troubles than to correct structural troubles.

Falsehoods which arise due to some irregularity in the application of the intellect are like functional trou-bles, and falsehoods which arise due to the vitiation of

Importance of purifying intellect

the intellect are like structural troubles. *Just as functional troubles are easier to correct than structural troubles, falsehoods arising out of irregu-larity in the application of the intellect are easier to correct than the falsehoods which arise due to the vitiation of intellect.* In order to correct the functional troubles of a vital organ all that is necessary is to give it a better tone and strength. If there is a structural trouble it is often necessary to perform an operation. In the same way, if falsehoods arise due to some mistakes in the application of the intellect, all that is necessary is more *carefulness* in the application of the intellect; but if falsehoods arise due to vitiation of the intellect, it is necessary to *purify* the intellect. This requires the painful process of *cutting out those desires and attachments which are responsible for vitiating the intellect.*

The falsehoods of vitiated thinking spring from initial mistakes in valuation. They arise as a *side-product* of psychic activity, which consists in the pursuit of certain accepted values. They **Citadels of *Maya*** come into existence as a part of *rationalisation* and justification of the accepted values, and they owe their hold upon the human mind to their apparent support of those accepted values. If they did not affect human values or their realisation, they would immediately dwindle into insignificance and lose their grip upon the mind. When false beliefs derive their being and vitality from deep-rooted wishes they are nourished by false seeking. If the error in false beliefs is purely intellectual it is easy to set right. But *false beliefs which are nourished by false seeking are the citadels of Maya.* They involve much more than intellectual error, and are not diminished by mere counter-assertion of a purely intellectual nature.

Elimination of desires and attachments which vitiate thinking is not accomplished purely by sheer intellect. This requires right effort and right action. Not in **Clarity of perception from inner purity** arm-chair speculation, but in the doing of right things shall spiritual truths be discovered. Honest action is a preliminary to the elimination of spiritual falsehoods. The perception of spiritual truths requires not merely strenuous and furious thinking, but clear thinking, and *true clarity of thought is a fruit of a pure and tranquil mind.*

Not until the stripping off of the last vestige of *Maya*-created falsehood is God known as *the* Truth. Only when *Maya* is completely crossed does there arise the

God as Truth known after transcending falsehoods

supreme knowledge that God is the *only* Truth. God alone is real. All that is not God, all that is impermanent and finite, and all that seems to exist within the domain of duality is false. God is one Infinite Reality; all divisions which are conceived within this Reality are falsely conceived; they do not actually exist.

When God is considered as divisible it is due to *Maya.* The variegated world of multiplicity does not effect the partitioning of God into several different

God is indivisible

portions. There are different ego-minds, different bodies, different forms, but only one soul. *When the One Soul takes different ego-minds and bodies, there are different individualised beings,* but this does not introduce any multiplicity within the Soul itself. The Soul is and always remains indivisible. The one indivisible Soul is the base of the different ego-minds which do the thinking and acting of various types, and which go through innumerable types of dual experiences; but the one indivisible Soul is and always remains beyond all thinking and doing and beyond all dual experience.

Different opinion or different ways of thinking do not introduce multiplicity within the one indivisible

Differences of thinking create no divisions within Soul

Soul for the simple reason that there are no opinions or any ways of thinking within the Soul. All the activity of thinking and conclusions drawn are within the ego-mind, which is finite. *The soul does not think; it is only the ego-mind which thinks.* Thinking and the knowledge which comes through thinking are both possible in the state of imperfect and incomplete knowledge which belongs to finite ego-minds. In the soul itself there is neither thinking nor the knowledge that comes through thinking.

The soul is infinite thought and infinite intelligence, but there is no division between the thinker and the thinking and the conclusions of thinking, nor the duality of the subject and object. Only the

Soul is infinite thought and infinite intelligence

ego-mind with the background of the soul can become the thinker. The soul, which is infinite thought and infinite intelligence, does not think or have any activity of the intellect. Intellect and its limited thinking comes into existence only with the finite ego-mind. *In the completeness and sufficiency of the infinite intelligence, which is the Soul, there is no need for the intellect or its activities.*

With the shedding of the last vestige of falsehoods created by *Maya*, the soul not only knows its reality to be different from the gross, the subtle or the mental body,

God the only Reality

but it knows itself to be God, Who is the *only* Reality. It knows that the mind, the subtle body and the physical body were all equally the creations of its own imagination, that in reality they never existed, that it was through ignorance that it conceived *itself* as the mind or the subtle body or the physical body, and that it, as it were, itself became the mind, the subtle body or the gross body and *then* identified itself with all these *self-created illusions*.

Maya

GOD is infinite by being above the limiting opposites of duality. He is above the limited aspects of good and bad, small and great, right and wrong, virtue and evil, happiness and misery;

God beyond duality

therefore He is infinite. If God were good rather than bad or bad rather than good, or if He were small rather than great or great rather than small, or if He were right rather than wrong or wrong rather than right, or if He were virtuous rather than evil or evil rather than virtuous, or if He were happy rather than miserable or miserable rather than happy, He would be finite and not infinite. *Only by being above duality is God infinite.*

Whatever is infinite must transcend duality; it cannot be one part of duality. That which is truly infinite cannot be the dual part of the finite. *If the infinite is*

**Finite cannot be
second part of infinite**

regarded as existing side by side with the finite it is no longer infinite, for it then becomes the second part of duality. *God, Who is infinite, cannot descend into duality. So, the apparent existence of duality as infinite God and the finite world is illusory. God alone is real; He is infinite, One without a second.* The existence of the finite is only apparent; it is false; it is not real.

How does the false world of finite things come into existence? Why does it exist? It is *created by Maya* or the principle of ignorance. *Maya* is not illusion, it is the creator of illusion. *Maya* is not false, it is that which gives false impressions. *Maya is not unreal; it is that which makes the real appear unreal and the unreal appear real. Maya* is not duality, it is that which causes duality.

World of finite things a creation of *Maya*

For the purposes of intellectual explanation *Maya* must be looked upon as being infinite. *It creates the illusion of finitehood; it is not in itself finite.* All the illusions which are created by *Maya* are finite, and the entire universe of duality, which appears to exist due to *Maya,* is also finite. The universe may seem to contain innumerable things but that does not make it infinite. Stars may be countless; there are a huge number, but the total collection of stars is nevertheless finite. Space and time might seem to be infinitely divisible, but they are nevertheless finite. Everything which is finite and limited belongs to the world of illusion, but the principle which causes this illusion of finite things must, *in a sense,* be regarded as not being an illusion.

Creations of *Maya* are finite

Maya cannot be considered as being finite. A thing becomes finite by being limited in time. *Maya* does not exist in space and cannot be limited by it. *Maya cannot be limited in space, because space is itself the creation of Maya. Space, with all that it contains,* is an illusion and is dependent upon *Maya. Maya, however,* is in no way dependent upon space.

***Maya* not limited by space**

Hence *Maya* cannot be finite through any limitations of space.

Nor can *Maya* be finite because of any limitations of time. Though *Maya* comes to an end in the state of super-consciousness, it need not be considered finite for that reason. *Maya* cannot have

Maya not limited by time

a beginning or end *in* time, because time itself is a creation of *Maya*. Any view that makes *Maya* a happening that takes place at some time and disappears after some time, places *Maya* in time and not time in *Maya*. *Time is in Maya, Maya is not in time.* Time as well as all happenings in time are the creations of *Maya*. Time comes into existence because of *Maya* and disappears when *Maya* disappears. *God is a timeless reality and the realisation of God and the disappearance of Maya is a timeless act.* *Maya* is in no way limited by time.

Nor can *Maya* be considered to be finite for any other reasons, for if it were finite it would be an illusion, and being an illusion it would not have any potency to create other illusions. *For the*

Maya is infinite

purposes of intellectual explanation, Maya is best regarded as being both real and infinite, in the same way that God is usually regarded as being both real and infinite.

Among all possible intellectual explanations, the explanation that *Maya,* like God, is both real and infinite is most acceptable to the intellect of man. Nevertheless *Maya* cannot be *ultimately* true.

Maya cannot be ultimately true

Wherever there is duality there is finitehood on both sides. The one thing limits the other. There cannot be two real Infinites. There can be two *huge* things, but there cannot be two *infinite* entities. If we have the duality of God and *Maya* and if both are regarded as coordinate existents, then the infinite reality of God is considered as the second part of a duality. Therefore *the intellectual explanation that Maya is real does not have the stamp of final knowledge, though it is the most plausible explanation.*

There are difficulties in regarding *Maya* as illusory and also *as ultimately* real. Thus *all attempts of the limited intellect to understand Maya lead to an impasse.* On the

Intellectual difficulties in understanding Maya

one hand if *Maya* is regarded as finite, it itself becomes illusory and then it cannot account for the illusory world of finite things. Therefore *Maya* has to be regarded as being both real and infinite. On the other hand if *Maya* is regarded as being ultimately real, it itself becomes a second part of the duality of another infinite reality, namely God. From this point of view, therefore, *Maya* actually seems to become finite and therefore unreal. So, *Maya cannot be ultimately real though it has to be regarded as such in order to account for the illusory world of finite objects.*

In whatever manner the limited intellect tries to understand *Maya*, it falls short of true understanding. It is not possible to understand *Maya* through the limited

Maya is God's shadow

intellect; it is as unfathomable as God. *God is unfathomable, un-understandable; so is Maya unfathomable, un-understandable.* So they say, "*Maya* is God's shadow." Where a man is, there is his shadow also. So where God is, there is this inscrutable *Maya*.

Though God and *Maya* are inscrutable for the lim-

Enigma of Maya solved after realisation

ited intellect working under the domain of duality, they can be thoroughly understood in their true nature in the *final knowl-*

edge of realisation. The enigma of the existence of Maya can never be finally solved until after realisation, when it is known that Maya does not exist in reality.

Maya does not exist in two states. In the original *unconscious* state of Reality there is no *Maya* and in the *Self-conscious* or *super-conscious* state of God also

Maya does not exist in two states

there is no *Maya*. It exists only in God's consciousness of the phenomenal world of duality, *i.e.*, when there is consciousness of the gross world, or consciousness of the subtle world, or consciousness of the mental world. *Maya exists when there is no Self-consciousness but only consciousness of the imagined other, and when consciousness is helplessly dominated by the false categories of duality.*

Maya exists only from the point of view of the finite. *It is only in illusion that Maya exists as a real and infinite creator of unreal and finite things. From the point*

Maya exists only for illusion

of view of the last and the only Truth of realisation, nothing exists except infinite and eternal God. There the illusion of finite things as separate from God has vanished, and with it has also vanished Maya, the creator of this illusion.

Self-knowledge comes to the soul by looking within, and by crossing *Maya*. In that self-knowledge it not only knows that the different ego-minds and bod-

Knowledge of realisation

ies never existed, but also that the entire universe and Maya itself never existed as a *separate* principle. Whatever reality *Maya* ever had is now swallowed up in the indivisible being of the One Soul. *The Soul knows itself to be what it has always been—eternally Self-realised, eternally infinite in knowledge, bliss, power and existence, and eternally free from duality.* But this highest form of self-knowledge is inaccessible for the intellect, and it is incomprehensible except to those who have attained the heights of final realisation.

The Conditions of Happiness

PART I
REMOVAL OF SUFFERING
THROUGH DETACHMENT

EVERY creature in the world is seeking happiness, and man is no exception. Seemingly man sets his heart on many kinds of things, but all that he desires

Every man aims at happiness

or undertakes is for the sake of happiness. If he is keen about having power it is because he expects to derive happiness from its use. If he strives for money it is because he thinks it will secure for him the conditions and means for his happiness. If he seeks knowledge, health or beauty, science, art or literature, it is because he feels that his pursuit of happiness is directly dependent upon them. If he struggles for worldly success and fame it is because he hopes to find his happiness in their attainment. *Through all his endeavours and pursuits, man wants to be happy. Happiness is the ultimate motive-power which drives him in all that he does.*

Everyone seeks to be happy, yet most persons are immersed in some kind of suffering. If at times they do get small installments of happiness in their lives, it is neither unadulterated nor abiding. *Man's life is never*

Intertwining of pleasure and pain

a series of unmixed pleasures. It moves between the opposites of pain and pleasure which are entwined like darkened clouds and shining rainbows. The moments of pleasure occasionally appearing in the life of man soon vanish, like the rainbows, which shine in their splendour only to disappear from the sky. If these moments of pleasure leave any trace, it is of a memory which only augments the pain of having lost them. Such memory is an invariable legacy of most pleasures.

Man does not seek suffering; but it comes to him as an inevitable outcome of the very manner in which he seeks happiness. He seeks happiness through the fulfill-

Desire bears two kinds of fruit

ment of his desires, but such fulfillment is never an assured thing, hence in the pursuit of desires man is also unavoidably preparing for the suffering from their non-fulfillment. *The same tree of desire has two kinds of fruit: one sweet which is pleasure, and one bitter which is suffering.* If the tree is allowed to flourish it cannot be made to yield just one kind of fruit. The one who has bid for one kind of fruit must be ready to have the other also. Man pursues pleasure furiously and clings to it fondly when it comes. He tries to avoid impending suffering desperately, and smarts under it with resentment. His fury and fondness are not of much avail, for his pleasure is doomed to fade and disappear one day, and his desperation and resentment are equally of no avail, for he cannot escape the suffering that results.

Goaded by multifarious desires, man seeks the pleasures of the world with unabating hope. His zest

Changing moods

for pleasures does not remain uniform, however, because

even while he is reaching for the cup of pleasure, he often has to gulp down doses of suffering. His enthusiasm for pleasure is abated by suffering, which often follows in pleasure's wake. He is subject to sudden moods and impulses. Sometimes he is happy and elated, at other times he is very unhappy and down-hearted. His moods change as his desires are fulfilled or frustrated. *Satisfaction of some desires yields momentary happiness, but this happiness does not last, and it soon leads to the reaction of depression.* His moods subject him to ups and downs and to constant change.

Fulfillment of desires does not lead to their termination; they are submerged for awhile only to reappear with added intensity. When a person is hungry he eats

Suffering caused by desires

to satisfy the desire, but soon feels hungry again. If he eats too much, even in the fulfillment of his desire he experiences pain and discomfort. It is the same with all the desires of the world; they can only yield a happiness which is fleeting. Even in the very moment of fulfillment the happiness they yield has already begun to fade and vanish. *Worldly desires can therefore never lead to abiding happiness. On the contrary, they invariably invite unending suffering of many kinds.* When man is full of worldly desires a plentiful crop of suffering is unavoidably in store for him. Desire is inevitably the mother of much suffering; this is the law.

If a person experiences or visualises the suffering which waits upon desires his desires become mitigated. Sometimes intense suffering makes him detached from

Mitigation of desires through sight of suffering

worldly life, but this detachment is often again set aside by the fresh flood of desires. Many persons temporarily lose their interest in worldly objects due to the impact of acute suffering brought on by desires, but detachment must be lasting if it is to pave the way for freedom from desires. There are *varying degrees of detachment*, but not all of them are lasting.

Sometimes a person is greatly moved by an unusually strong experience, such as seeing a corpse being carried to the burial ground, or seeing the corpse

Temporary detachment

being buried or burnt. Such experiences are thought-provoking and they initiate long trains of ideas about the futility and emptiness of worldly existence. Under the pressure of such experiences the person realises that one day he must die and take leave of all the worldly objects so dear to him. But such thoughts, as well as the detachment born thereof, are short-lived. They are soon forgotten and the person resumes his attachment to the world and its alluring objects. The temporary and passing mood of detachment is known as *Smashan-vairagya*, because it usually arises in the burial ground and stays in mind only in the presence of the corpse. *Such a mood of detachment is as temporary as it is sudden.* It seems to be strong and effective while it lasts, but it is only sustained by the vividness of some experience, and when the experience vanishes, the mood of detachment also quickly flitters away, without seriously affecting the general attitude towards life.

The passing mood of detachment might be illustrated by the story of a person who once saw at the theatre a spiritual drama about Gopichanda. The drama

Illustrative story

impressed him so deeply that, disregarding all his duties to his family, he joined a band of *Bairagis* (wandering ascetics) belonging to the cult of Gopichanda. Renouncing all his former modes of life he dressed as a *Bairagi,* shaved his head and sat under a tree, as advised by the other members of the group. At first he plunged into deep meditation, but as the heat of the sun grew stronger his enthusiasm for meditation began to cool down. As the day went on he began to feel hungry and thirsty and became very restless and miserable. When the members of his family noticed his absence from home they became worried about him. After some searching they found him sitting under the tree in this miserable plight. He had grown haggard and was plainly unhappy. His wife seeing him in this strange condition was furious and rushed to upbraid him. His mood of detachment had flitted away, and as he was thoroughly tired of his new life, he took her approach as a boon from heaven. So, silencing her quickly, he put on his *pagri* and ordinary clothes and meekly followed her home.

Sometimes the mood of detachment is more lasting and not only endures for a considerable time, but also seriously modifies one's general attitude towards

Intense detachment   life. This is called *Tivra-vairagya* or intense dispassion. Such intense dispassion usually arises from some great misfortune—such as the loss of one's own dear ones or the loss of property or reputation. Under the influence of this wave of detachment the person renounces all worldly things. *Tivra-vairagya* of this type has its own spiritual value, but it is also likely to disappear in the course of time, or be upset by the onset of a recurring flood of worldly desires. The disgust for the world which a person feels in such cases is due to a powerful impression left by a misfortune, and it does not endure because it is not born of understanding. It is only a severe *reaction* to life.

The kind of detachment which really lasts is due to the understanding of suffering and its cause. It is securely based upon the unshakable knowledge that all things of

Complete detachment

this world are momentary and passing and that any clinging to them is bound eventually to be a source of pain. Man seeks worldly objects of pleasure and tries to avoid things that bring pain without realising that he cannot have the one and eschew the other. As long as there is attachment to worldly objects of pleasure he must perpetually invite upon himself the suffering of not having them, and the suffering of losing them after having got them. Lasting detachment which brings freedom from all desires and attachments is called *Purna-vairagya* or complete dispassion. Complete detachment is one of the essential conditions of lasting and true happiness, for he who has complete detachment no longer creates for himself the suffering which is due to the unending thraldom produced by desires.

Desirelessness makes a man firm like a rock. He is neither moved by pleasure nor by sorrow; he is not upset by the onslaughts of opposites. He who is affected

Opposites

by agreeable things is bound to be affected by disagreeable things. If a person is encouraged in his endeavours by an omen considered auspicious, he is bound to be discouraged by an omen considered to be inauspicious. He cannot remain proof against the discouraging effect of an inauspicious omen as long as he derives strength from the auspicious omen. The only way not to be upset by omens is to be indifferent to auspicious as well as inauspicious omens.

The same is true of the opposites of praise and blame. If a person is pleased by receiving praise he is bound to be miserable when he receives blame. He can-

Praise and blame

not keep himself steady under a shower of blame as long as he is inwardly delighted by receiving praise. *The only way not to be upset by blame is to be detached from praise also.* Only then can a person remain unmoved by the opposites of praise and blame. Then he does not lose his equanimity. The steadiness and equanimity which remain unaffected by any opposites is possible only through complete detachment, which is an essential condition of lasting and true happiness. He who has complete detachment is not at the mercy of the opposites of experience, and being free from the thraldom of all desires, he no longer creates his own suffering.

Man is subject to many sufferings, physical and mental. Of these two, mental suffering is the more acute. Those with limited vision think that suffering can only

Physical and mental suffering

be physical. Their idea of suffering is of some kind of illness or torture of the body. *Mental suffering is worse than physical suffering.* Physical suffering sometimes comes as a blessing because it serves the purpose of easing mental suffering by weaning away man's attention from the mental suffering.

It is not right to make much of purely physical suffering. It can be borne through the exercise of will-power and endurance. The true suffering that counts is

Abiding happiness through desireless-ness

mental, and even yogis who can endure great physical suffering find it difficult to keep free from mental suffering which is rooted in the frustration of desires. If a man does not want anything he is not unhappy under any adverse circumstances, not even in the jaws of a lion. The state of complete desirelessness is *latent in every one,* and when, through complete detachment, one reaches the state of wanting nothing, one taps the unfailing inner source of eternal and unfading happiness which is not based upon the objects of the world, but is sustained by self-knowledge and self-realisation.

The Conditions of Happiness

MOST of man's suffering is self-created through his ungoverned desires and impossible demands. All this is unnecessary for self-fulfillment. If man becomes desireless and contented he will be free from his self-inflicted suffering. His imagination will not be constantly harassed by feverish reaching out towards things that really do not matter, and he will be established in unassailable peace. *When man is contented he does not require any solutions to problems, because the problems which confront worldly persons have disappeared.* He *has* no problems, therefore he does not have to worry about their solution. For him the complexities of life do not exist, because his life becomes utterly simple in the state of desirelessness.

Contentment cuts out harassment of self-created problems

When a person understands desires as being merely the bondage of the spirit, he decides to give them up; but even when voluntary, this is often a painful process. The suffering that comes from purging the mind of its many desires exists, even

Suffering of renunciation

when the soul may be ready to renounce them, because this decision of the soul goes counter to the inclination of the ego-mind to persist through its habitual desires. *Renunciation of desires curtails the very life of the ego-mind. Therefore it is a process invariably accompanied by acute suffering.* But such suffering is wholesome for the soul because it liberates the soul from bondage.

Not all suffering is bad. When suffering leads to the eternal happiness of desirelessness, it should be regarded as a blessing in disguise. Just as a patient may have to suffer an operation at the hands of a surgeon in order

Analogies

to free himself of persistent and malignant pain, the soul has to welcome the suffering of renouncing desires in order to be free from the recurrent and unending suffering caused by them. The suffering which the soul has in renouncing desires may be very acute, but *it is endured because of a sense of greater freedom which comes when desires gradually disappear from the mind.* If a swelling on the body is opened and allowed to drain it gives much pain, but also much relief. Similarly, the suffering from renunciation of desires is accompanied by the compensating relief of progressive initiation into the limitless life of freedom and happiness.

The simple life of freedom and happiness is one of the most difficult things to achieve. Man has complicated his life by the growth of artificial and imaginary desires, and returning to sim-

Unification through suffering

plicity amounts to the renunciation of desires. Desires have become part and parcel of the limited self of man, with the result that he is reluctant to abandon them unless the lesson that desires are born of ignorance is impressed upon his mind through acute mental suffering.

When a man is confronted with great suffering through his desires, he understands their true nature. When such suffering comes it should be welcomed. Suffering may come in order to eliminate further suffering. A thorn may be taken out by another thorn, and suffering by suffering. Suffering has to come when it is of use in purging the soul of its desires; it is then as necessary as medicine to a sick man.

However, ninety-nine percent of human suffering is not necessary. Through obstinate ignorance people inflict suffering upon themselves and their fellowmen, and then, strangely enough, they ask, "Why should we suffer?" Suffering is generally symbolised by scenes of war: devastated houses, broken and bleeding limbs, the agonies of torture and death; but war does not embody any *special* suffering. *People really suffer all the time. They suffer because they are not satisfied—they want more and more. War is more an outcome of the universal suffering of dissatisfaction than an embodiment of representative suffering.* Through his greed, vanity and cruelty, man brings untold suffering upon himself and others.

Chief suffering is discontent

Man is not content to create suffering only for himself, but he is relentlessly zealous in creating suffering for his fellowmen. Man seeks his own happiness even at the cost of the happiness of others, thus giving rise to cruelty and unending wars. As long as he thinks only of his own happiness he does not find it. In the pursuit of his own individual happiness the limited self of man becomes accentuated and burdensome. *When man is merely selfish he can, in the false pursuit of separate and*

Selfish pursuit of happiness makes man callous

exclusive happiness, become utterly callous and cruel to others, but this recoils upon him by poisoning the very spring of his life. Loveless life is most unlovely, only a life of love is worth living.

If a man is desireless he will not only eliminate much suffering which he causes others, but also much of his own self-created suffering. Mere desirelessness,

Happiness through self-forgetful love

however, cannot yield positive happiness, though it protects man from self-created suffering and goes a long way towards making true happiness possible. *True happiness begins when a man learns the art of right adjustment to other persons, and right adjustment involves self-forgetfulness and love.* Hence arises the spiritual importance of transforming a life of the limited self into a life of love.

Pure love is rare, because in most cases love becomes adulterated with selfish motives which are surreptitiously introduced into consciousness by the

Sefless love is rare

operation of accumulated bad *sanskaras. It is extremely difficult to purge consciousness of deep-rooted ignorance that expresses itself through the idea of "I" and "mine."* For example, even when a man says that he wants his beloved, he often means that he wants his beloved to be with him. The feeling of "I" and "mine" is notably present even in the expression of love. If a man sees his own son wearing tattered clothes, he does all that he can to give him good clothes and will be anxious to see him happy. Under these circumstances he would consider his own feeling towards his son as that of pure love. But, in his quick response to the distress of his son, the part played by the idea of "mine" is by no means inconsiderable. If he happened to see the son of some stranger on the street wearing tattered clothes, he would not respond as he had in the case of his own son. This shows that though he may not be fully conscious of it, his behaviour towards his own son was, in fact, largely selfish. The feeling of "mine" is there in the *background* of the mind, though it can be brought to the surface only through searching analysis. If his response to the son of the stranger is the same as to his own son, then only can he be said to have pure and selfless love.

Pure love is not a thing that can be forced upon someone, nor can it be snatched away from another by force. It has to manifest from within with unfettered spontaneity. What *can* be achieved through bold decision is the removal of those factors which prevent the manifestation of pure love. The achievement of selflessness may be said to be *both difficult and easy.* It is difficult for those who have not decided to step out of the limited self, and it is easy for those who have so decided. In the absence of firm determination, attachments connected with the limited self are too strong to break through, but if a person resolves to set aside selfishness at any cost, he finds an easy entry into the domain of pure love.

Pure love easy and difficult

The limited self is like an external coat worn by the soul. Just as a man may take off his coat by the exercise of will, so through a bold decisive step he can make up his mind to shed the limited self and get rid of it once and for all. The task which otherwise would be difficult becomes easy through the exercise of *bold and unyielding decision.* Such decision can be born in his mind only when he feels an intense longing for pure love. Just as a man who is hungry longs

Need for bold decision

for food, so the aspirant who wants to experience pure love has an intense longing for it.

When the aspirant has developed this intense longing for pure love he may be said to have been prepared for the intervention of the Master who, through proper direction and necessary help, ushers him into the state of divine love. Only a Master can awaken love through the divine love which he imparts; there is no other way. *Those who want to be consumed in love should go to the eternal flame of love.* Love is the most significant thing in life. It cannot be awakened except by coming into contact with the Incarnation of Love. Theoretical brooding on love will result in weaving a *theory* about love, but the heart will remain as empty as before. *"Love begets love;" it cannot be awakened by any mechanical means.*

True love awakened only by Master

When true love is awakened in man it leads him to the realisation of God and opens up an unlimited field of lasting and unfading happiness. The happiness of God-realisation is the goal of all creation. It is not possible for a person to have the slightest idea of that inexpressible happiness without actually having the experience of Godhood. The idea which the worldly man has of suffering or happiness is entirely limited. *The real happiness which comes through realising God is worth all the physical and mental suffering in the universe. Then all suffering is as if it had never been.*

Love leads to God-realisation

Even those who are not God-realised can control their minds through *yoga* to such an extent that nothing makes them feel pain or suffering, even if they are buried or thrown into boiling oil. But though the advanced *yogis* can brave and annul any suffering, they

Happiness of God-realisation unlimited and permanent

do not experience the happiness of realising God. When one becomes God, everything else is zero. The happiness of God-realisation, therefore, does not suffer curtailment by anything. *The happiness of God-realisation is self-sustained, eternally fresh and unfading, boundless and indescribable. It is for this happiness that the world has sprung into existence.*

God as Infinite Love

THOSE who try to understand God through the intellect alone, arrive at some cold and dry concept which misses the very essence of the nature of God. It is

Essence of God is love

true that God is infinite knowledge, infinite existence, infinite power and infinite bliss, but God is not understood in His essence until He is also understood as *infinite love.* In the Beyond State from which the entire universe springs and into which it ultimately merges, God is *eternally* infinite love. It is only when God's love is viewed in the limited context of *forms* (which arise in the interim period of the appearance of the illusory universe of duality) that its infinity *seems* to have been impaired.

When God's love experiences itself *in* and *through* the manifested forms of the universe, it goes through the following phases: (i) experiencing itself as extremely

Course of manifest love

limited, (ii) experiencing itself as becoming less and less limited and becoming more and more like infinite love, and (iii) experiencing itself to be what it really is: infinite in essence and existence. *The experience of limitation in love arises due to ignorance caused by the sanskaras (which are the by-product of the evolution of consciousness); and the process of love be-*

coming infinite is characterised by the shedding of these limiting sanskaras.

After going through the almost unconscious stages of the mineral kingdom, love becomes conscious of itself as lust in animals. Its first appearance in human

Love as lust

consciousness is also in the form of lust. *Lust is the most limited form of love in human consciousness. In spite of the clear reference which lust has to other persons, it is indistinguishable from undiluted selfishness, because all the objects to which lust clings are desired for the sake of and from the viewpoint of the limited and separate self.* At the same time, it is a form of love, because it has in it some kind of appreciation for others, though this appreciation is completely vitiated by thick ignorance about the true Self.

When human consciousness is completely caught up in the duality of the *gross* sphere of existence, love cannot express itself as anything other than lust of some

Love in gross sphere

type. A man likes curry because it tickles his palate. There are no higher considerations, so it is a form of lust. It is only a craving for the sensations of taste. Mind also has cravings for the bodily sensations of sight, smell, sound and touch, and nourishes its crude ego-life through the excitement derived from these sensations. *Lust of every type is an entanglement with gross forms, independent of the spirit behind them. It is an expression of mere attachment to the objects of sense. Since in all forms of lust the heart remains unfed and unexpressed, it becomes a perpetual vacuum and is in a state of unending suffering and non-fulfillment.*

Love, which expresses itself as *undiluted* or one hundred per cent lust, is in a state of extreme limitation because it is helplessly caught up in ceaseless craving.

Lust is extreme limitation

When the heart is in the clutches of lust, the spirit remains, as it were, in a state of delusion or stupor. Its functioning is severely curtailed and perverted by the limiting ignorance to which it is subject. Its higher potentialities are denied expression and fulfillment, and this thwarting and suppression of the life of the spirit entails a state of utter bondage.

Lust is the most limited form of love functioning under the thraldom of ignorance. The unambiguous stamp of insufficiency which lust invariably bears

In lust self-assertion of infinity is indirect

is in itself a sign that it is an incomplete and inadequate expression of something deeper, which is vast and unlimited. *Through the manifold and unending sufferings which are attendant upon undiluted lust, and the continued experiences of frustration which it brings, the spirit is ceaselessly registering its unyielding protest against the utter superficiality of a life of unqualified lust. In this manner the irrepressible voice of the infinity of God's love indirectly asserts the imperative claims of its unexpressed but unimpaired reality.*

Even in the lowest lustful life of the *gross* sphere, God is experiencing Himself as a lover, but it is a state of a lover who is completely ignorant about the true nature

Three stages of the lover

of himself or the beloved. It is a state of a lover who is inexorably separated from the beloved by an opaque curtain of un-understood duality. It is nevertheless the beginning of a long process by which *the lover breaks through the enveloping curtain of ignorance and comes into his own Truth as unbounded and unhampered Love.* But in order to get initiated into infinite love, the lover has to go through two other stages which are characteristic of the *subtle* and *mental* spheres.

The lover in the *subtle* sphere is not free from lust, but the lust which he experiences is not undiluted as in the gross sphere. The intensity of lust in the subtle sphere is about half that in the gross sphere. Besides, there is no gross expression of lust as in the gross sphere. The lover in the gross sphere is inextricably entangled with the gross objects; hence his lust finds gross expression. But the lover in the subtle sphere has gotten free from attachment to gross objects; hence in his case lust remains unexpressed in the gross form. His lust has *subtle* expressions, but it cannot have gross expression. Besides, since about half of the original lust of the gross sphere gets sublimated in the subtle sphere, the lover in the subtle sphere experiences love not as undiluted lust, but in a higher form as *longing to be united with the Beloved.*

Love in subtle sphere

Thus in the gross sphere love expresses itself as lust, and in the subtle sphere it expresses itself as *longing.* Lust is a craving for sensations and as such is completely selfish in motive. It has utter disregard for the well-being of the beloved. In longing there is less of selfishness, and though it continues to be *possessive* in a way, the beloved is recognised as having worth and importance in his own right. Longing is a less limited form of love than lust. In longing the curtain of duality has become more transparent and less obstructive, since the lover now consciously seeks to overcome duality between the lover and the Beloved by securing the presence of the Beloved. *In lust the emphasis is solely on the limited self and the beloved is completely subsidiary to the gross needs*

Love as longing

of the self. In longing the emphasis is equally distributed on the self and on the beloved, and the lover realises that he exists for the beloved just in the same way as the beloved exists for him.

The lover in the *mental* sphere has an even higher and freer expression of love. In his case, though lust has not completely disappeared, it is mostly sublimated. Only about one-fourth of the original lust of the gross **Love in mental sphere** sphere remains, but it remains in a latent form without any expression. *In the mental sphere, lust does not have even subtle expression.* The lover of the mental sphere is detached from subtle objects, and he is *free from possessive longing for the beloved* which is characteristic of the lover in the subtle sphere.

In the mental sphere love expresses itself as *complete resignation to the will of the beloved.* All selfish desire, including longing for the presence of the beloved, has disappeared. Now the emphasis is solely on the worth **Love as resignation** and will of the beloved. Selfishness is utterly wiped out and there is a far more *abundant release of love in its pure form.* However, even in the mental sphere love has not become infinite, since there is still present the thin curtain of *duality* which separates the lover from the beloved. Love is no longer in the clutches of selfishness, but it is still short of being infinite because it is *experienced through the medium of the finite mind,* just as in the lower spheres it is experienced through the medium of the lower bodies.

Love becomes consciously infinite in being as well as in expression, when the individual mind is transcended. Such love is rightly **Divine love is infinite** called divine, because it is characteristic of the God-state in which all duality is finally overcome. In divine love, lust has completely disappeared. It does not exist even in latent form. *Divine love is unlimited in essence and expression, because it is experienced by the soul through the soul itself.* In the gross, subtle and mental spheres the lover is conscious of being separated from the beloved, but when all these spheres are transcended, the lover is conscious of his unity with the Beloved. The lover loses himself in the being of the Beloved and knows that he is one with the Beloved. Divine love is entirely free from the thraldom of desires or limiting self. *In this state of infinity the lover has no being apart from the Beloved. He is the Beloved Himself.*

We thus have God as infinite love, first limiting Himself in the forms of creation, and then recovering His infinity through the different stages of creation.

The divine romance   All the stages of God's experience of being a finite lover ultimately culminate in His experiencing Himself as the sole Beloved. *The sojourn of the soul is a thrilling divine romance in which the lover, who in the beginning is conscious of nothing but emptiness, frustration, superficiality and the gnawing chains of bondage, gradually attains an increasingly fuller and freer expression of love, and ultimately disappears and merges in the divine Beloved to realise the unity of the Lover and the Beloved in the supreme and eternal fact of God as Infinite Love.*

Twelve Ways of Realising Me

1. LONGING   If you experience that same longing and thirst for union with me as one who has been lying for days in the hot sun of the Sahara experiences the longing for water, then you will realise me.

2. PEACE OF MIND   If you have the peace of a frozen lake, then too you will realise me
.

3. HUMILITY   If you have the humility of the earth which can be moulded into any shape, then you will know me.

4. DESPERATION   *If you experience the desperation that causes a man to commit suicide and you feel that you cannot live without seeing me, then you will see me.*

5. FAITH   If you have the complete faith that Kalyan had for his Master, in believing it was night although it was day (because his Master said so), then you will know me.

6. FIDELITY   If you have the fidelity that the breath has in giving you company, even without your constantly feeling it, till the end of your life (that both in happiness and in suffering gives you company and never turns against you), then you will know me.

7. *CONTROL THROUGH LOVE* When your love for me drives away your lust for the things of the senses, then you will realise me.

8. *SELFLESS SERVICE* If you have the quality of selfless service unaffected by results, similar to that of the sun which serves the world by shining on all creation—on the grass in the field, on the birds in the air, on the beasts in the forest—on all mankind with its sinner and its saint, its rich and its poor, unconscious of their attitude towards it, then you will win me.

9. *RENUNCIATION* If you renounce for me everything physical, mental and spiritual, then you have me.

10. *OBEDIENCE* If your obedience is as spontaneous, complete and natural as the light is to the eye or the smell to the nose, then you come to me.

11. *SURRENDERANCE* *If your surrenderance to me is as whole-hearted as that of one who, suffering from insomnia, surrenders to sudden sleep without fear of being lost, then you have me.*

12. *LOVE* If you have that love for me which St. Francis had for Jesus, then not only will you realise me but you will please me.

Books by Meher Baba

God Speaks
In God's Hand
The Everything and the Nothing
Listen Humanity
Beams from Meher Baba
Life at its Best
Discourses